Culture of Honor

New Directions in Social Psychology
Richard E. Nisbett, Series Editor

Social psychology is moving in new directions as the root questions of culture, group structure, communication, collective representations, and societal conflict are being answered in innovative ways. The new social psychology not only employs the conceptual and methodological tools of social cognition but in asking broader questions often draws on sociology, political science, history, philosophy, and anthropology. By using this interdisciplinary approach, social psychologists are mapping out ways to understand the role groups play in influencing individual minds. New Directions in Social Psychology brings the best of this work together in an effort to shape and advance these emerging trends.

Culture of Honor: The Psychology of Violence in the South,
Richard E. Nisbett and Dov Cohen

Individualism and Collectivism, *Harry C. Triandis*

**Justice, Liability, and Blame: Community Views
and the Criminal Law,** *Paul H. Robinson and John M. Darley*

FORTHCOMING

Social Psychology and Law, *Eugene Borgida*

Cultural Psychology of African Americans, *James M. Jones*

Culture and Interpersonal Morality, *Joan Miller*

Faces: Appearance, Social Perception, and Human Development,
Leslie A. Zebrowitz

CULTURE OF HONOR

The Psychology of Violence in the South

Richard E. Nisbett
Dov Cohen

A Member of the Perseus Books Group

New Directions in Social Psychology

Copyright © 1996 by Westview Press, A Member of the Perseus Books Group

Published in 1996 in the United States of America by Westview Press, Inc., 5500 Central Avenue, Boulder, Colorado 80301-2877, and in the United Kingdom by Westview Press, 12 Hid's Copse Road, Cumnor Hill, Oxford OX2 9JJ

A CIP catalog record for this book is available from the Library of Congress.
ISBN-10: 0-8133-1993-5   ISBN-13: 978-0-8133-1993-3

The paper used in this publication meets the requirements of the American National Standard for Permanence of Paper for Printed Library Materials Z39.48-1984.

Contents

Illustrations

Figures

Tables

Acknowledgments

THE WORK REPORTED in this book was made possible by grants from the National Science Foundation, the Russell Sage Foundation, and the Office of the Vice President for Research of the University of Michigan.

Thanks are due to many people who made this project possible.

For their thoughtful discussions and stimulating ideas: Brian Bowdle, David Buss, Jim Dabbs, Martin Daly, Phoebe Ellsworth, Alan Fiske, Sam Gross, Kent Harber, Lawrence Hirschfeld, Hazel Markus, Andrew Reaves, Lee Ross, Norbert Schwarz, Dan Sperber, J. E. Keith Smith, Leigh Ann Vaughn, Margo Wilson, and Piotr Winkielman.

For their outstanding work in the design and execution of the project and for making it fun to work on: Mechele de Avila, Jessica Berns, Carissa Bowles, Terri Brandes, Mary Cullen, Wendy Dodrill, David Dulio, Amie Eigner, Jennifer Euster, Nancy Exelby, Ed Ferrer, Athena Foley, Tangie Fry, Becky Gastman, Cory Hardy, David Howell, Kerrie Johnson, Stephanie Kitchen, Andrea Kozak, Fred Lennox, Sheri Levy, Karla Metzger, David Mosby, Kristen Nimelli, Sean O'Neil, Sangita Patel, Holly Pesavento, Chris Powers, Jasmin Riad, Frank Rowan, Jeremy Shook, Cassie Slisher, Pam Smith, Jon Steinfeld, Kevin Taylor, Ken Visser, Dottie Walker, Tomica Williams, and Phil Wills.

And—most important—for their love, support, wisdom, and faith: our friends and families, to whom this book is dedicated.

Richard Nisbett
Dov Cohen

Introduction

THIS IS A BOOK ABOUT a singular cause of male violence—the perpetrator's sense of threat to one of his most valued possessions, namely, his reputation for strength and toughness. In many of the world's cultures, social status, economic well-being, and life itself are linked to such a reputation. This is true wherever gaining resources, or keeping them, depends on the community's believing that the individual is capable of defending himself against predation. If resources are abundant or are not subject to theft (like those of most traditional farming peoples, for example), then a reputation for toughness has little value. But if resources are in scarce or unpredictable supply, and if they are sufficiently portable that theft is a practicable route to bounty, then toughness has great economic value. Potential predators will go elsewhere rather than risk dealing with a man who knows how to defend himself and his possessions and who appears to be not afraid to die.

What have the above observations to do with violence in the U.S. South? A great deal, in our view. The South has long been thought to be more violent than the North, and we believe that some distinctive aspects of the South are key to this violence. Unlike the North, which was settled by farmers from England, Holland, and Germany, the South was settled by herdsmen from the fringes of Britain. Herdsmen the world over tend to be capable of great aggressiveness and violence because of their vulnerability to losing their primary resources, their animals. Also, unlike the North, where population densities have been in general relatively high, the South was a low-population frontier region until well into the nineteenth century. In such regions the state often has little power to command compliance with the law, and citizens have to create their own system of order. The means for doing this is the rule of retaliation: If you cross me, I will punish you.

To maintain credible power of deterrence, the individual must project a stance of willingness to commit mayhem and to risk wounds or death for himself. Thus, he must constantly be on guard against affronts that could be construed by others as disrespect. When someone allows himself to be insulted, he risks giving the impression that he lacks the strength to protect what is his. Thus the individual must respond with violence or the threat of violence to any affront.

Anthropologists call the kind of culture just described a "culture of honor." They use *honor* not in the sense of probity of character but in the sense of status and power. The thesis of this book is that the South had—and to a substantial degree still has—a type of culture of honor. If we could avoid using this term, we would, both because it is not clear to the layperson just what sort of "honor" is meant and because we have found that anthropologists bristle at the term *culture of honor* applied to anything in the United States. For anthropologists, the typical culture of honor is a Mediterranean village where the individual lives in a small face-to-face community that he will never leave. In such a culture, honor is not merely a self-defense concern: It suffuses all relations. A person sits in the proper pew or not; and his daughter marries well or badly, depending on his honor. In contrast, all regions of the United States are considered far too individualistic to be cultures of honor in this sense. But saying that the southern United States has a culture of honor is merely asserting that the South shares many properties with other cultures of honor. One of those properties is the necessity for men to appear strong and unwilling to tolerate an insult.

We hope this book will provide much that is of interest for both the layperson and the social scientist concerning violence and a particular culture that gives rise to it. For the social scientist, however, the book is also about something more important. It is about the once and future discipline of *cultural psychology*. As such it offers our vision of what the field should be—methodologically and theoretically.

Several decades ago there was a field called "culture and personality." It generated some extremely valuable work, such as Margaret Mead's studies of gender, which showed that gender roles and relations were not entirely determined by biology but rather differed greatly across cultures; Ruth Benedict's work systematically describing Japanese culture and comparing it with Western culture; and John and Bea Whitings' demonstrations of differential socialization patterns for children living in societies having different economies and values. This work is among the most impressive in all social science, but it had come to an end by the 1960s. We believe there were several reasons for this. One was ideological: In an era that favored psychological and cultural universalism, it became inappropriate to imply that human groups were different in any important sense. A second was metatheoretical: There was no set of principles that could tell the investigator where the "fault lines" of cultures would be, that is, which dimensions would show the biggest and theoretically most important differences and which aspects would be universal. The third was methodological: The tools used by the early investigators were primarily the ethnographer's observations and various personality tests that many social scientists would now regard as being of limited validity even within our own culture.

All three of these factors are now radically different, opening up the possibility of a principled, scientific field of cultural psychology that will have no apologies to make. First, the ideological barriers are gone. Today there is great interest in cultural differences. As the United States in particular becomes ever more diverse, and as various ethnic groups demand attention and respect in part because of their very differences from mainstream culture, the study of cultural difference gains acceptability, even necessity.

Second, there is, we believe, an emerging metatheoretical base for the social sciences that is particularly relevant to cultural studies. This base is the set of principles underlying evolutionary psychology. Evolutionary psychology encourages us to differentiate between (1) problems that all human groups have had to solve (for example, rearing young who are not self-sufficient for many years, regulating sexual behavior within the social unit, and so on) and (2) problems that are presented by varying ecologies, economies, and political situations. The former, universal sort of problems should probably yield constant cross-cultural adaptations, whereas the latter should yield novel adaptations affecting social structure and individual psychology in ways that make sense for local requirements. Thus we may soon have a principled guide as to where to look for universalities and for cultural differences, as well as what the nature of the differences should be.

The third point is one of the major messages of this book: In our view, the scientific study of culture in the "culture and personality" era was hampered by reliance on too narrow a range of methodologies. In addition to the methods of the ethnographer and the psychometrician, it is possible to apply the methods of the historian, the "cliometrician" (quantitative and archival studies of history and social institutions), the survey sociologist, and the experimental social psychologist. When all of these methods are used to study the same set of problems and when they point toward the same conclusions, a level of inference can be achieved that is far beyond what investigators could have accomplished at an earlier time.

We have applied this panoply of methods to questions concerning violence and the culture of honor. Making use of the historical and ethnographic work of others, we have drawn a picture of traditional, herding-based cultures of honor around the world and shown their commonalities with the historical and contemporary cultures of the U.S. South. With archival methods using census and crime reports, we have collected evidence showing that the homicide rate of the South, especially the rural South, remains high relative to the rest of the country. Using survey techniques, we have collected evidence indicating that the values of southerners favor violence for purposes of protection of property, for retaliation for an insult, and for the socialization of children. Employing experimental methods, we have collected evidence showing that southerners respond to insults in ways that are cognitively, emotionally, physiologically, and behaviorally quite different from the pattern shown by northerners. In field experiments, we have shown that southern institutions are more accepting of individuals who have committed violent crimes in defense of their honor. And with archival methods, we have collected evidence indicating that many of the social institutions and contemporary public policies of the South have their roots in the culture of honor—including the acceptance of violence to protect property and personal and national honor.

The body of evidence in this short book, we believe, presents an overwhelming case for a difference between cultures that one normally thinks of as being essentially similar—the southern and northern United States. It is perhaps precisely because of this presumption of similarity, which undoubtedly does exist for most attributes, that the present case for cultural difference seems particularly striking.

1

Violence and Honor in the Southern United States

THE U.S. SOUTH HAS LONG BEEN viewed as a place of romance, leisure, and gentility. Southerners have been credited with warmth, expressiveness, spontaneity, close family ties, a love of music and sport, and an appreciation for the things that make life worth living—from cuisine to love.

But there has also been the claim that there is a darker strain to southern life. For several centuries, the southern United States has been regarded as more violent than the northern part of the country.[1] This belief has been shared by foreign visitors, northerners, and southerners with experience outside the South. Duels, feuds, bushwhackings, and lynchings are more frequently reported in the correspondence, autobiographies, and newspapers of the South than of the North from the eighteenth century on.[2] The rates of homicide in some areas of the South in the nineteenth century make the inner city of today look almost like a sanctuary. According to one accounting, in the plateau region of the Cumberland Mountains between 1865 and 1915, the homicide rate was 130 per 100,000[3]—more than ten times today's national homicide rate and twice as high as that of our most violent cities.

Not only homicide but also a penchant for violence in many other forms are alleged to characterize the South. The autobiographies of southerners of the eighteenth and nineteenth centuries often included accounts of severe beatings of children by parents and others.[4] And southern pastimes and games often involved violence that is as shocking to us today as it was at the time to northerners. In one game called "purring," for example, two opponents grasped each other firmly by the shoulders and began kicking each other in the shins at the starting signal. The loser was the man who released his grip first.[5] Even more horrifying to modern (and to contemporaneous northern) sensibilities was a favorite sport of frontiersmen called fighting "with no holds barred," which meant that weapons were banned but nothing else was. Contestants

1

could and did seek to maim their opponents.[6] Thus gouged-out eyes and bit-ten-off body parts were common outcomes of such fights.

Cases of southern violence often reflect a concern with blows to reputation or status—with "violation of personal honor"—and the tacit belief that violence is an appropriate response to such an affront. The journalist Hodding Carter has written that in the 1930s he served on a jury in Louisiana that was hearing a case concerning a man who lived next to a gas station where the hangers-on had been teasing him for some time. One day he opened fire with a shotgun, injuring two of the men and killing an innocent bystander. When Carter proposed a verdict of guilty, the other eleven jurors protested: "He ain't guilty. *He wouldn't of been much of a man if he hadn't shot them fellows.*"[7] A historian has written of the same period that it was impossible to obtain a conviction for murder in some parts of the South if the defendant had been insulted and had issued a warning that the insult had to be retracted.[8] And until the mid-1970s, Texas law held that if a man found his wife and her lover in a "compromising position" and killed them, there was no crime—only a "justifiable homicide."

The young men of the South were prepared for these violent activities by a socialization process designed to make them physically courageous and ferocious in defense of their reputations: "From an early age small boys were taught to think much of their own honor, and to be active in its defense. Honor in this society meant a pride of manhood in masculine courage, physical strength and warrior virtue. Male children were trained to defend their honor without a moment's hesitation."[9]

Even very young children were encouraged to be aggressive, learning that "they were supposed to grab for things, fight on the carpet to entertain parents, clatter their toys about, defy parental commands, and even set upon likely visitors in friendly roughhouse."[10] Children themselves rigorously enforced the code of honor. A boy who dodged a stone rather than allow himself to be hit and then respond in kind ran the risk of being ostracized by his fellows.[11]

The southerners' "expertise" in violence is reflected in their reputed success as soldiers.[12] Southerners have been alleged, at least since Tocqueville's commentary on America, to be more proficient in the arts of war than northerners and to take greater pride in their military prowess. Twentieth-century scholars have documented the southern enthusiasm for wars, their overrepresentation in the national military establishment, and their fondness for military content in preparatory schools and colleges.[13]

Explanations for Southern Violence

There are many "Souths"—the Cavalier South of seventeenth- and eighteenth-century Virginia, founded by the inheritors of the medieval knightly tradition of horsemanship and skill in battle; the mountain South, originating in eastern

Appalachia and moving southward and westward decade by decade; the plantation South, based on growing cotton; and the western South, based on the herding of cattle in dry plains and hills that could sustain no other form of agriculture. Of the explanations that we will cite for southern violence, certain ones apply plausibly to some of these regions but less plausibly to others.

Four major explanations have been offered for the southern tendency to prefer violence: the higher temperature of the South and consequently the quicker tempers of southerners, the tradition of slavery, the greater poverty of the South, and the putative "culture of honor" of the South. We argue that the role of "honor" is independent of, and probably greater than, any role played by the other three.

Temperature. It has been suggested that at least a part of the violence of the South can be accounted for by the characteristically higher temperatures of the South.[14] It is indeed possible to show that variation in temperature in a locality is associated with the number of violent crimes there,[15] and we will examine the role played by temperature in the most dramatic form of violence, namely homicide.

Slavery. Slavery has long been held responsible for the violence of the South.[16] Abigail Adams was of the opinion that whites inflicted on themselves the same sort of violent treatment that they accorded their slaves.[17] Thomas Jefferson concurred, in his *Notes on Virginia,* as did many other thoughtful southerners. John Dickinson, an eighteenth-century revolutionary from the eastern shore of Maryland, believed that the institution of slavery led to southern "pride, selfishness, peevishness, violence."[18] Tocqueville also believed that slavery was responsible for the South's violence, but he emphasized, rather than the "contagion" from treatment of the slaves, the idleness encouraged by slavery:

> As [the Kentuckian] lives in an idle independence, his tastes are those of an idle man . . . and the energy which his neighbor devotes to gain turns with him to a passionate love of field sports and military exercises; he delights in violent bodily exertion, he is familiar with the use of arms, and is accustomed from a very early age to expose his life in single combat.[19]

At several points in this book we will assess the evidence for and against both aspects of slavery as explanations for southern violence.

Poverty. A third explanation for the greater violence of the South has to do with poverty. The South is poorer than any other region of the country and always has been; in each region of the country and in every sort of population unit, from rural county to large city, poverty is associated with higher homicide rates.

A variant of the economic explanation focuses not on absolute income or wealth but rather on disparities in income. Some argue that inequality in wealth breeds violence. We will attempt to assess the role of poverty and inequality in the violence of the South both in rates of homicide and in preference for violence as a means of conflict resolution.

Violence and the Culture of Honor

We believe that the most important explanation for southern violence is that much of the South has differed from the North in a very important economic respect and that this has carried with it profound cultural consequences. Thus the southern preference for violence stems from the fact that much of the South was a lawless, frontier region settled by people whose economy was originally based on herding. As we shall see, herding societies are typically characterized by having "cultures of honor" in which a threat to property or reputation is dealt with by violence.

Virtue, Strength, and Violence

Cultures of honor have been independently invented by many of the world's societies. These cultures vary in many respects but have one element in common: The individual is prepared to protect his reputation—for probity or strength or both—by resort to violence. Such cultures seem to be particularly likely to develop where (1) the individual is at economic risk from his fellows and (2) the state is weak or nonexistent and thus cannot prevent or punish theft of property. And those two conditions normally occur together: Herding, for example, is the main viable form of agriculture in remote areas, far from government enforcement mechanisms.

Some cultures of honor emphasize the individual's personal honesty and integrity in the sense that honor is usually meant today. That has always been one of the major meanings of the concept. Dr. Samuel Johnson, the eighteenth-century compiler of the first English dictionary, defined honor as "nobility of soul, magnanimity, and a scorn of meanness." This is "honour which derives from virtuous conduct."[20] Honor defined in those terms is prized by virtually all societies; the culture of honor, however, differs from other cultures in that its members are prepared to fight or even to kill to defend their reputations as honorable men.

The culture of honor also differs from others in an even more important respect. In addition to valuing honor defined as virtuous conduct, it values—often far more—honor defined as respect of the sort "which situates an individual socially and determines his right to precedence."[21] Honor in this sense is based not on good character but on a man's strength and power to enforce his will on others. Again, almost all societies value honor defined as precedence or status. The culture of honor differs from other cultures in that violence will be used to attain and protect this kind of honor. Honor, as we use the term in this book, is well captured by ethnographer David Mandelbaum's characterization of the Arabic and Persian word for honor—*izzat*. "It is a word often heard in men's talk, particularly when the talk is about conflict, rivalry, and struggle. It crops up as a kind of final explanation for motivation, whether for acts of aggression or beneficence."[22]

A key aspect of the culture of honor is the importance placed on the insult and the necessity to respond to it. An insult implies that the target is weak enough to be bullied. Since a reputation for strength is of the essence in the culture of honor, the individual who insults someone must be forced to retract; if the instigator refuses, he must be punished—with violence or even death. A particularly important kind of insult is one directed at female members of a man's family.

> In the Old South, as in the ancient world, "son of a bitch" or any similar epithet was a most damaging blow to male pride. . . . To attack his wife, mother, or sister was to assault the man himself. Outsider violence against family dependents, particularly females, was a breach not to be ignored without risk of ignominy. An impotence to deal with such wrongs carried all the weight of shame that archaic society could muster.[23]

Herding Economies and the Culture of Honor

The absence of the state makes it possible for an individual to commit violence with impunity, but it is not a sufficient condition for creating a culture that relies on violence to settle disputes. Hunting-gathering societies appear to have relatively low levels of violence, even though their members are not usually subjects of any state.[24] And farmers, even when they live in societies where the state is weak, typically are not overly concerned with their reputation for strength nor are they willing to defend it with violence.[25]

Herding and Vulnerability to Loss. There is one type of economy, however, that tends to be associated worldwide with concerns about honor and readiness to commit violence to conserve it. That is the economy based on herding of animals.[26] Together with some anthropologists, we believe that herding societies have cultures of honor for reasons having to do with the economic precariousness of herdsmen.[27] Herdsmen constantly face the possibility of loss of their entire wealth—through loss of their herds. Thus a stance of aggressiveness and willingness to kill or commit mayhem is useful in announcing their determination to protect their animals at all costs.

Herding and Sensitivity to Insults. Herdsmen adopt a stance of extreme vigilance toward any action that might imply that they are incapable of defending their property. Early in his career, in fact, the herdsman in some cultures may deliberately pick fights to show his toughness. As the ethnographer J. K. Campbell wrote of Mediterranean herding culture:

> The critical moment in the development of the young shepherd's reputation is his first quarrel. Quarrels are necessarily public. They may occur in the coffee shop, the village square, or most frequently on a grazing boundary where a curse or a stone aimed at one of his straying sheep by another shepherd is an insult which inevitably requires a violent response.[28]

Herding and the Uses of Warfare

People who herd animals usually live in places such as mountains, semideserts, and steppes, where because of the ecology, crop farming is inadequate to provide for basic food needs. They have little surplus and sometimes experience genuine want. Thus they are often tempted to take the herds of other groups. As a consequence, "theft and raiding are endemic to pastoral peoples."[29] Or, as one herdsman of the Middle East put it, "Raids are our agriculture."[30] Thus skill at warfare is valuable to a herdsman in a way that it is not to a hunter-gatherer or a farmer. It is no accident that it is the herding peoples of Europe who have been reputed to be the best soldiers over the centuries, that "to the Scots, as to the Swiss, Swedes, Albanians, Prussians and other people of Europe's margins and infertile uplands, war has been something of a national industry."[31]

In addition to the "marginal" northern Europeans, many if not most Mediterranean groups—including the traditional cultures of such peoples as the Andalusians of southern Spain, the Corsicans, Sardinians, Druze, Bedouins, Kabyle of Algeria, and Sarakatsani of Greece—are characterized as holding to a version of the culture of honor.[32] These groups all have economies that are greatly dependent on herding. Many other traditional societies of Africa[33] and the steppes of Eurasia and North America[34] also have (or had) herding economies and cultures of honor.

There are some interesting natural experiments that show that people who occupy the same general region but differ in occupation also differ in their predilections toward toughness, violence, and warfare. Anthropologist Robert Edgerton studied two neighboring tribes in East Africa, each of which included a group of herders and a group of farmers. Edgerton reported that in both tribes, the pastoralists exhibited "a syndrome that can best be described as *machismo*," whereas farmers manifested "the insistent need to get along with . . . neighbors."[35]

In North America, the Navajo and the Zuni also inhabit similar ecological niches, but the Navajo are herders and the Zuni are farmers. The Navajo are reputed to be great warriors (right up to the present—they served in large numbers and with distinction in World War II). The Zuni are more peaceable and have not been noted as warriors at any time in their history.[36]

An even better natural experiment came with the introduction of the horse to the American Indians of the Plains. Prior to the arrival of the horse, the tribes of the Plains had been relatively peaceful; after its introduction, many tribes began to behave like herders everywhere. They reckoned their wealth in terms of the number of horses they owned, they staged raids on their neighbors, and they began to glorify warfare.[37]

Herding and the Weakness of the State

Since herding usually takes place in regions where geography and low population density conspire against the ability of law enforcement officials to reach their targets, defense against enemies is left up to the individual and the small community in which he lives. For many people in such circumstances, the prevailing form of law is the feud—with the threat of deadly consequences for family members as the primary means of maintaining order. Hence it should be no surprise that the feuding societies of the world are preponderantly herding societies.[38]

The Scotch-Irish and the Herding Economy in Europe and America

What has the reputed violence of the U.S. South to do with the culture of honor as it might be evidenced by a Greek shepherd, an East African warrior, or a Navajo? In our view, a great deal.

The northern United States was settled by farmers—Puritans, Quakers, Dutch, and Germans. These people were cooperative, like farmers everywhere, and modern in their orientation toward society. They emphasized education and quickly built a civilization that included artisans, tradespeople, businesspeople, and professionals of all sorts.

In contrast, the South was settled primarily by people from the fringes of Britain—the so-called Scotch-Irish.[39] These people had always been herders because the regions where they lived—Ireland, Scotland, Wales—were not in general suitable for more-intensive forms of agriculture.[40]

The Celts and Their Descendants

The Scottish and the Irish were descendants of the Celts, who had kept cattle and pigs since prehistoric times and had never practiced large-scale agriculture.[41] Like other herding peoples, the Celts reckoned their wealth in terms of animals, not land, and were accustomed to intertribal warfare and cattle raiding.[42] The Romans feared the Celts because of their ferocity (though the Romans were not impressed with the Celts' organizational abilities). Over centuries of war, including Julius Caesar's famous battles with the Gauls, the Celts were driven into Britain. Subsequent wars—with Vikings, Danes, Angles, Saxons, and other Germanic peoples—drove them to the least hospitable fringe areas. The battles really never ceased, however, especially along the Scottish frontier with England and between the Scottish and Irish in Ulster.

One cannot know how relevant the distant past of this culture is. But it may be worth noting that the Celtic peoples did not develop the characteristics of farmers until their emigration to America.[43] They did not undergo the transformation common elsewhere in Europe from serf to peasant to bourgeois farmer. When they engaged in agriculture at all, it was generally of the horticultural or slash-and-burn variety in which a field was cultivated for three or four years and then left to lie fallow for a decade or more.[44] Such a method is the most efficient one when, as is true in most of the range of the Celtic peoples, the soil is unproductive. An important characteristic of this method of farming is that it does not encourage permanence on the land. Periodic movement was common,[45] a fact to bear in mind when one contemplates the behavior of the Scotch-Irish after they came to America.

The Scotch-Irish in the U.S. South and West

The immigration of the Scotch-Irish to North America began in the late seventeenth century and was completed by the early nineteenth century. The group was composed largely of Ulster Scots, Irish, and both lowland and highland Scots.[46] The impoverished, deeply Roman Catholic Irish who came later in the nineteenth century, as well as the Presbyterian, often highly educated Scots, were culturally very different from these earlier immigrants, who were both more secular and more inclined to violence as a means of settling disputes.[47]

Their new land, if anything, served to reinforce the herding economy practiced by the Scotch-Irish immigrants.[48] With its mountains and wide-open spaces, America, especially the Appalachians and the South, was ideally suited to the herding life and to horticulture.[49] The Scotch-Irish tended to seek out relatively unproductive lands to homestead, but even when they found themselves on highly productive land, they tended to farm in low-efficiency, horticultural fashion rather than in the more efficient agrarian manner that involves clearing the land of stumps, rotating crops, and making the sort of improvements that would have made movement away from the land hard to contemplate.[50]

The geography and low population density probably served to increase culture-of-honor tendencies in another respect as well: Because of the remoteness and ruggedness of the frontier, the law was as weak in America as it had been in Britain: "In the absence of any strong sense of order as unity, hierarchy, or social peace, backsettlers shared an idea of order as a system of retributive justice. The prevailing principle was *lex talionis,* the rule of retaliation."[51] Or, as a

North Carolina proverb stated, "Every man should be sheriff on his own hearth."

The southerner, thus, was of herding origin, and herding remained a chief basis of the economy in the South for many decades. Not until the invention of the cotton gin in the early nineteenth century would there be a viable economic competitor to herding. The cotton gin made possible the plantation South. But by the early nineteenth century, the characteristic cultural forms of the Celtic herding economy were well established, and at no time in the nineteenth century did southern folkways even in the farming South converge on those of the North.[52]

When we refer to "the South" in this book, we always mean to include the states of the deep South as well as the mountain states of Tennessee, Kentucky, and West Virginia; but many of our generalizations hold, often with equal force, to the West. The herding economy moved with the Scotch-Irish to the West— that is, to Texas and Oklahoma and the mostly southern portions of the mountain West that were settled by southerners. Again, the herding economy was basic because of the ecology. Thus, it should not be surprising that the westerner, like the southerner, shared the common characteristics of herding peoples everywhere: He used violence to protect his herd and his property; he was hypersensitive to insult because of its implications for his strength and ability to defend himself; he was skilled in the arts of combat; and he was careful to train his children, especially boys, to be capable of violence when needed.

Though we have relied on the findings of the ethnographer and historian, their methods are limited in their capacity to address these issues. Even the best-considered assertions by scholars can be challenged as mistaken subjective interpretations by other scholars. Moreover, quantitative social scientists themselves have presented conflicting evidence. Some maintain, on the basis of one type of data or another, collected by one method or another, that there is no culture of honor, no greater violence, and no attitudinal network supportive of violence existing in the South today—if there ever was.

In this book we examine a very wide array of data concerning many topics related to the culture of honor, using archival, survey, experimental, and field-experimental methods. We believe that the great bulk of this evidence speaks with a single voice: The South retains a version of the culture of honor, and this culture is largely responsible for the greater violence of the region.

In Chapter 2, we examine the question of contemporary homicide rates in the South. We try to establish that rates of homicide for non-Hispanic whites are higher there and that no "structural" reason offered to date, for example, poverty or income inequality, or "artifactual" reason, for example, presence of guns, can account for this difference. Moreover, we show that the differences in homicide rate between North and South are greater for small cities and the countryside than they are for big cities, which supports the view that it is rural, ecological, and agricultural differences that contribute most to the homicide differences between regions.

In Chapter 3 we show that attitudes of contemporary southerners toward violence are specific in their focus, that is, southerners do not support violence of all kinds but precisely the sorts of violence that the culture of honor would be expected to promote. Southerners, as compared to northerners, are more inclined to favor violence when it is for protection of property, or as a response to an insult, or as a means of socializing children.

Chapter 4 provides a very different line of evidence concerning our central thesis: We examine the response of southerners and northerners to insults in controlled laboratory experiments. We show that after being insulted, southern subjects express more anger than do northern subjects, undergo more hormonal changes indicative of stress and preparation for aggression, act more aggressively against another individual, and express more dominance. In addition, the insulted southerner believes that the affront diminishes him in the eyes of others much more than the northerner does.

Chapter 5 presents evidence that many of the laws and social policies of the South reflect the individual attitudes examined in surveys in Chapter 3 and revealed in behavior in the laboratory in Chapter 4. For example, southern states are found to have laws and social policies that are more lenient with regard to self-defense, gun control, corporal punishment, and capital punishment. Southern statutes reflect a greater acceptance of violence for protection, honor, and maintaining control than do northern statutes. The chapter concludes with two field experiments showing that institutions in the South and West stigmatize honor-related violence less than those of the North.

In Chapter 6 we summarize the evidence in favor of a culture-of-honor explanation of southern violence and argue that this evidence is more convincing than that supporting various other explanations. We compare the southern culture of honor with other cultures that currently are mired in violence, including the inner cities of the United States. The chapter also examines the role of women both as participants and as socialization agents in cultures of honor.

Finally, Chapter 6 asks what will happen to the culture of honor in the South. Will it wither away—as a Marxist materialist account would be obliged to predict—since few people in the South today are in any danger of having their herds stolen? Or on the contrary, will it retain its strength or even grow? Several factors, ranging from the functional autonomy of socially sanctioned behavior to the allure of the "smile when you say that" stance, suggest that the culture of honor may remain strong for some time.

A final note on what this book is *not* about: Since it is concerned with a negative aspect of the U.S. South—namely, its high level of violence—there is a risk that it will be perceived in some sense as an attack on southern culture. That it most certainly is not. In fact, the explanation that we offer for southern violence tends both to make its origins seem rational and its eventual demise ap-

pear likely. The book makes no attempt to be an ethnography of southern culture in any broad sense. Such ethnographies exist, and they argue very persua-
sively that there is a southern culture—or rather many southern cultures—differing substantially from what most people take to be mainstream U.S. culture.
To us, personal experience and balanced cultural accounts make it clear that
there is much that is distinctive and highly attractive about the U.S. South. Indeed, in our experience it is the rare visitor to the South who does not quickly
see some of these distinctive aspects or who leaves the South without wishing
that some of them could be taken home.

Notes

1. Gastil, 1989, p. 1473.
2. Fischer, 1989; Redfield, 1880, cited in Gastil, 1989, p. 1473.
3. Caudill, 1962, p. 46.
4. Fischer, 1989, p. 689.
5. McWhiney, 1988, p. 154.
6. Gorn, 1985, p. 20.
7. Carter, 1950, p. 50, emphasis in original.
8. Brearley, 1934.
9. Fischer, 1989, p. 690.
10. Wyatt-Brown, 1982, p. 138.
11. McWhiney, 1988, p. 203.
12. Napier, 1989.
13. May, 1989, p. 1108.
14. Anderson, 1989.
15. Anderson, 1989; Cotton, 1986; Reifman, Larrick, and Fein, 1991; Rotton and
Frey, 1985.
16. Gastil, 1971.
17. Ammerman, 1989, p. 660.
18. Quoted in Wyatt-Brown, 1982, p. 153.
19. Tocqueville, [1835] 1969, p. 379.
20. Johnson, 1839.
21. Pitt-Rivers, 1965, p. 36.
22. Mandelbaum, 1988, p. 20.
23. Wyatt-Brown, 1982, p. 53.
24. Farb, [1968] 1978; O'Kelley and Carney, 1986.
25. Edgerton, 1971; Farb, [1968] 1978, pp. 121–122.
26. Edgerton, 1971, pp. 16–17; Farb, [1968] 1978, pp. 9–10; Galaty, 1991, p. 188;
Lowie, 1954; Peristiany, 1965, p. 14.
27. See, for example, O'Kelley and Carney, 1986, pp. 65–81.
28. Campbell, 1965, p. 148.
29. O'Kelley and Carney, 1986, p. 65.
30. Black-Michaud, 1975, p. 199.
31. Keegan, 1944, p. 167.

32. Black-Michaud, 1975; Gilmore, 1990; Peristiany, 1965; Fisek, 1983.
33. Galaty and Bonte, 1991.
34. Lowie, 1954; Farb, [1968] 1978.
35. Edgerton, 1971, pp. 18, 297.
36. Farb, [1968] 1978, pp. 258–259.
37. Farb, [1968] 1978, p. 9–10; Lowie, 1954.
38. Black-Michaud, 1975.
39. Fischer, 1989; McWhiney, 1988; Wyatt-Brown, 1982, p. 38.
40. Blethen and Wood, 1983, p. 7.
41. Chadwick, 1970, p. 25; McWhiney, 1988, p. xxiv.
42. Corcoran, 1970, p. 25; Chadwick, 1970, p. 37.
43. Cunliffe, 1979, p. 198.
44. Blethen and Wood, 1983, p. 20.
45. McWhiney, 1988, p. 9.
46. Fischer, 1989, pp. 613–634; McWhiney, 1988, p. xli.
47. McWhiney, 1988, esp. pp. xxxvii and xli.
48. McWhiney, 1988, pp. xli ff; Wyatt-Brown, 1982, p. 36.
49. Fitzpatrick, 1989, p. 71.
50. Blethen and Wood, 1983, p. 20.
51. Fischer, 1989, p. 765.
52. Fischer, 1989.

2

Homicide Rate Differences Between North and South

I N THE SOUTH, as in the United States generally, most homicides take place between acquaintances and a very high fraction of homicides occur in the context of arguments.[1] Many of these violence-provoking incidents, moreover, revolve around rather trivial-sounding issues.[2] As one Dallas homicide detective put it: "Murders result from little ol' arguments over nothing at all. Tempers flare. A fight starts, and somebody gets stabbed or shot. I've worked on cases where the principals had been arguing over a 10 cent record on a juke box, or over a one dollar gambling debt from a dice game."[3]

Regional Differences in Homicide Rates

But such behavior is not so irrational as it might at first seem. In many societies, insults and affronts involve high personal stakes. Such challenges are not usually offered lightly or thoughtlessly, and the failure to answer them can have serious costs in terms of reputation. That was true in the Old South,[4] and we suggest it is still true to some degree today. We suspect that lethal violence—particularly that stemming from insults and status contests—will be more common in the modern South than elsewhere. These assertions lead us to the following predictions:

1. Homicide rates will be higher for whites in the South than in the North.
2. North-South differences will be particularly dramatic for whites in smaller cities and rural areas, where the differences between herding and farming cultures have been more pronounced historically. Differences between North and South will be less dramatic in larger cities, which are less tied to agricultural concerns and reflect more industrial, cosmopolitan, and homogenizing influences.

3. Homicide rates for blacks will be unrelated to region. The great black migrations to northern cities are a relatively recent phenomenon,[5] and there is no reason to assume that anything like the long-standing cultural differences with regard to violence for whites living in different regions will characterize blacks in different regions. Our theory holds that homicide differences reflect cultural differences arising from economic and historical conditions, not just from living above or below the Mason-Dixon line.

4. *Within* the South, the herding versus farming history of the region will be important. Herding regions, because of the cultures of honor that are developed or maintained within them, will have higher homicide rates than farming regions.

5. The murder rate will be elevated primarily for argument- or conflict-related homicides, where insults and concern with damage to reputations are present. The rate of homicides committed merely for instrumental reasons, in the course of robbery or some other felony, will not be elevated in the South.

To test these hypotheses, Nisbett, Polly, and Lang[6] compiled homicide data from the *Supplementary Homicide Reports* for 1976–1983.[7] These reports break down the homicide data by race and circumstances (arguments, felonies, and so on). The homicide rates of cities of different sizes, in different regions, of non-Hispanic whites, and of blacks were examined.

Previous Studies of Regional Differences in Homicide

Since the ground-breaking work of Gastil[8] and Hackney,[9] many homicide researchers have believed that regional culture is an important variable. But other researchers believe the relationship between region and homicide is slight or fully explained by variables other than cultural ones. Their conclusions are based on regression analyses in which the region variable is usually included in the standard package of demographic variables, such as percent nonwhite, poverty, and city size.[10]

Researchers generally find that southernness has a slight to moderate correlation with homicide that is substantially diminished or even eliminated when they attempt to "control" for other variables in such regression analyses. However, we believe that such studies do not actually tell us much about southern culture and its relation to homicide. Specifically, previous studies have made two serious errors in examining the relation of southernness to homicide.

First, they have analyzed data at too high a level of aggregation—examining only states or large cities, when there is good theoretical reason to examine cities of all sizes and, moreover, to examine them *separately*.[11] Second, and perhaps more important, previous studies have aggregated all homicides, white and nonwhite, and then attempted to correct for this by including percent non-white as a predictor variable. Theoretically this method is unsound if one is trying to examine white culture of the North and South. Obviously, white homicide—not all homicide—should be the variable of interest.

For statistical reasons, it is also important to examine white rates separately because the percent of nonwhites is higher in the South and the percent of nonwhites is also correlated with homicide rate.[12] As several authors[13] have pointed out, this type of situation can cause one to dramatically underestimate the power of a variable like southernness, which is highly correlated both with homicide rate and with some other predictor variables, for example, percent nonwhite. Thus, it is essential to analyze the white homicide data separately rather than using data for the two races together and then attempting to take out the effects of race by statistical means.

Disaggregating Homicide Data

To disentangle the data, we conducted a study in which we examined homicide rates based on detailed U.S. Department of Justice data.[14] Two different types of rates are reported for the time period 1976–1983: (1) for males alone, the rate of murder and nonnegligent homicide *offenders;* and (2) for both sexes, the rate of murder and nonnegligent homicide *victims.* We report homicide rates for a sample of cities of size 10,000–50,000, 50,000–200,000, and more than 200,000, based on the 1980 census.[15]

We used the following variables in our analyses: Gastil's index of "southern-ness," that is, the percent of the initial settlers of a given state who were of southern origin; poverty; the GINI index of income inequality; population density; and the percent of males age 15 to 29 in the white non-Hispanic population. Details on the definitions of these variables can be found in Appendix A.

It may be seen in Figure 2.1 that white homicide rates differ greatly between North and South. Homicide rates are given as frequencies per 100,000 in the sample of each region. For ease of presentation, we clustered homicide rate

---

*The states included in each of the regions are as follows: New England (CT, MA, ME, NH, RI, VT), the Mid-Atlantic region (NJ, NY, PA), the Midwest (IA, IL, IN, KS, MI, MN, MO, NB, ND, OH, SD, WI), the Pacific region (CA, OR, WA), the Mountain region (AZ, CO, ID, MT, NM, NV, UT, WY), the Southwest (AR, LA, OK, TX), and the South (AL, DE, FL, GA, KY, MD, MS, NC, SC, TN, WV, VA). The South was defined as it was in the other chapters in this study, as census divisions 5, 6, and 7.

16

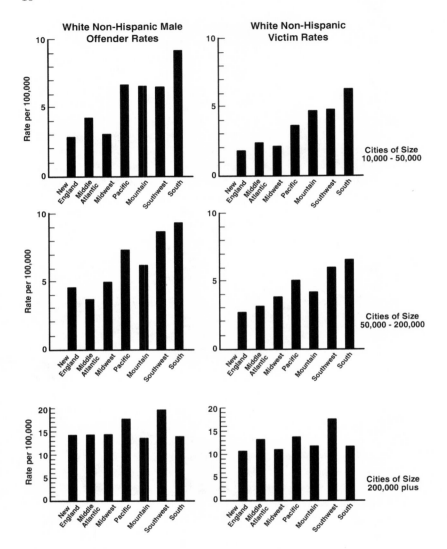

FIGURE 2.1 White non-Hispanic male homicide offender rates and white non-Hispanic homicide victim rates (per 100,000 of population) for cities of three different sizes. Source: Fox and Pierce, 1987.

data for the forty-eight contiguous states into seven different regions and listed the regions in order of their southernness as defined by Gastil's index.°

There is no regional difference at the very largest city sizes (over 200,000 in population), according to Figure 2.1, whereas differences between the South and New England of more than two to one obtain for cities between 50,000 and 200,000 and more than three to one obtain for cities between 10,000 and 50,000. There are comparable differences for the combined southern and southwestern states versus the combined eastern and midwestern states. The fact that smaller city sizes are associated with greater North-South differences is consistent with the notion that the regional differences are due to differences in the form of agriculture, since smaller cities are in general more reflective of rural culture.

There is nothing peculiar about our data set or form of analysis that might cause us to get results drastically different from those of other investigators. On the contrary, when we analyze the data the way others do, we find the same things. That is, when we aggregate the data across city size and race, we find moderate correlations between southernness and homicide rates. But when we subject this highly aggregated data to regression, the effect of southernness is greatly diminished, after controlling for variables like poverty and percent black.[16] It is only when we separate the data by race and city size that we can see the true effects of southern white culture.

Differential Predictions for Whites and Blacks and for Small and Large Cities

We have seen that there is a sizable relationship for whites between region and homicide. But there is *no* relationship between region and homicide rates for blacks at all, except for a small one for offender rates for the smallest cities. A similar point can be made for city size. As have other investigators, we found moderate correlations between southernness and homicide rates when medium and large cities were examined together, but that is misleading. There is a moderate correlation between southernness and homicide rates for medium-size cities (and for small cities), but essentially no correlation for the very largest cities.

Our analyses actually underestimate the relationship between southernness and homicide for whites, because of the systematic error that comes from defining predictor variables (like poverty and population density) over the whole population and not for whites only. When we examine white homicide data for cities that are 90 percent or more white and non-Hispanic, we lessen this error. Relationships between region and homicide rate for whites are stronger when only cities that are overwhelmingly white are examined. Thus, when we examine white homicide rates, we see that the impact of the southernness variable is quite important, remaining strong even after regression analyses and demonstrating the effect that is obscured by analysis of highly aggregated data. For detailed information on our statistical analysis, see Tables A.3 and A.4 in Appendix A.

Homicide Within the South: Where, What, and Why

Homicide Rates and Land Use

To link homicide rates more directly to agricultural practices, our colleague Andrew Reaves[17] examined homicide rates of different regions within the South. The most rural counties of the South were studied—all those having no town with a population of more than 2,500. Reaves looked at white, non-Hispanic male offender rates and also examined per capita income of the white population, population density, mean July temperature, percent of the population that is African-American, and percent of the population that was slave in 1860.

Counties were categorized as one of two kinds on the basis of their likely use for farming or herding. In general, the moist plains areas of the South allow for farming and cash crops, and the hills, defined as having an average slope of 8 percent or more, and the dry plains, having a precipitation rate of 24 inches or less, are more appropriate for herding.

As would be expected by the herding-culture-of-honor hypothesis, white male homicide rates are substantially higher in the hills and dry plains regions (12.27 homicides per 100,000) than in the farming regions (4.98 per 100,000), as may be seen in Figure 2.2. Two factors—slavery and hotter temperatures—are rendered relatively implausible as explanations, since they are in the wrong direction to explain the results. Slavery is associated with the moist plains because, of course, it was there that cotton could be grown successfully and that slavery was economically viable. However, it is in the hills and dry plains, where slavery was relatively uncommon, that homicide is higher today. The temperature is lower on average in the hills and dry plains than in the moist plains, but it is in the latter areas that homicide is more common. Poverty is a conceivable explanation of homicide differences. However, regional differences are small, and when regression analyses are conducted, the contribution of region remains highly significant even after income is controlled for.

In addition to southern rural counties, Reaves also examined white non-Hispanic male homicide rates for all comparably rural counties in New England, the Middle Atlantic states, and the states of the nonindustrial, western Midwest (North Dakota, South Dakota, Nebraska, and Kansas). The homicide rates are far higher for the southern counties—8.77 per 100,000—than for the northern counties—2.13 per 100,000. That is a ratio of slightly more than four to one and constitutes another indication that the smaller and more rural the population unit, the greater the homicide rate differences between North and South.

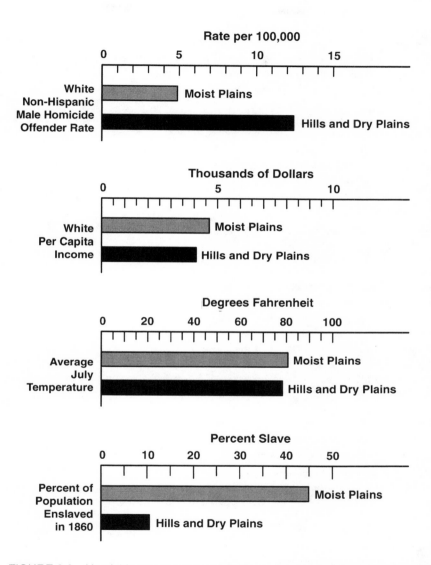

FIGURE 2.2 Homicide rates, per capita income, July temperature, and percent of population enslaved in 1860, in the moist plains and in the hills and dry plains of the South. Source: Reaves, 1993; Reaves and Nisbett, 1995.

Conflict-Related Versus Felony-Related Homicides

If it is the residue of the culture of honor that fuels high homicide rates in the South, one would expect that argument- and conflict-related homicide, as opposed to felony-related homicide, would be more common in the South. The argument- or conflict-related homicides are the ones that should involve issues of honor and protection at their base.

The Fox and Pierce *Supplementary Homicide Reports* code homicides in such a way that one may classify them as argument- or conflict-related (for example, brawls, lovers' triangles) versus felony-related (for example, homicides occurring in the context of a robbery or burglary). We added together all plausibly argument-related homicide categories and then all homicides clearly occurring in the context of some other felony, and we compared the two sorts of homicide statistics for the South and Southwest to statistics for other regions of the country.

Figure 2.3 indicates that white male offender homicide rates in smaller cities in the South and Southwest are elevated only for argument-related murders. The interaction based on raw frequencies is highly statistically significant. For larger cities, there are more argument-related homicides proportionately in the South and Southwest and fewer felony-related homicides, so the same interaction obtains, again highly significant.

Other investigators have come up with similar findings; they have shown that only homicides involving people personally known to the perpetrator are elevated in the South.[18] As the sociologist John Reed said, "The southerner who can avoid both arguments and adultery is as safe as any other American, and probably safer."[19] We will find yet more evidence of the southerner's selective views on the appropriateness of violence in Chapter 3.

Gun Ownership

One frequently offered and plausible explanation for the higher rate of homicide in the South is that southerners are more likely to own guns and hence to have ready access to a lethal weapon if they become angered. Although this might reflect a cultural difference (that is, a higher interest in guns in the South than in the North), it would scarcely be very interesting if it were the sole explanation for homicide rate differences.

Southerners are indeed more likely to own guns than northerners are. National Opinion Research Council surveys show that about two-thirds of all southern white men own guns, whereas only about 50 percent of northern white men do.[20] That cannot be the whole explanation of homicide differences, however. Even where gun ownership rates are equal, there are huge discrepancies between southern and northern homicide rates. As we found in a survey of rural counties of the South and Midwest, residents of both regions were equally (and overwhelmingly) likely to own guns.[21] But, as just indicated, in this

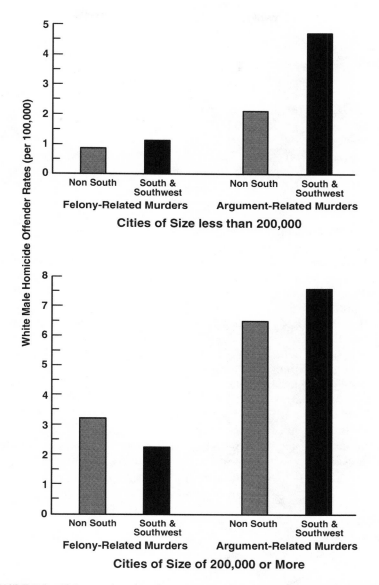

FIGURE 2.3 Felony-related and argument-related homicides committed by white males in cities of different sizes in the South and Southwest and in the Non South. Source: Fox and Pierce, 1987.

sort of rural county, there is a difference in homicide rate of three or four to one between South and North.

Culture and Homicide

In this chapter we established that there is indeed a higher rate of homicide in the South than in the North, and we have been able to cast substantial doubt on some of the chief explanations of this fact. Slavery is an improbable explanation because it is in the nonslave regions of the South that homicide rates are highest today. Temperature is not likely to explain much of the phenomenon for two reasons. First, it is the cooler regions of the South that have the higher homicide rates. Second, larger population units show little regional difference in homicide rates, whereas smaller population units show large regional differences. But both big cities and small are warmer in the South than in the North; thus it seems unparsimonious to invoke temperature to explain the regional differences for small cities. Finally, though the data certainly do not rule out poverty as an explanation of the homicide rate differences, they give no support to the view that poverty could be the sole explanation. Poverty is a predictor of homicide rate, but no better a predictor than region (see Appendix A, Table A.4), and the regional effect is highly significant even when poverty is controlled for.

In support of the cultural view we favor, we have shown that homicides, especially those involving arguments, are more common in the South, and that the more rural areas and those most suitable for herding are the ones that show the highest rates of homicide. For blacks, there is little regional difference in homicide rate, suggesting that it is something about white southern culture instead of just living below the Mason-Dixon line that drives the difference.

However, those results cannot establish conclusively that it is southern culture, rather than something else correlated with southernness, that affects white homicide rates. To give a convincing cultural explanation for the southern homicide phenomena, we need to go beyond culture as a mere "residual" explanation and show that there is something special about southern culture that might lead to the homicide difference. To do that, we will have to examine attitudes, beliefs, and behaviors concerning honor, self-protection, and violence.

Notes

1. Reed, 1981; Simpson, 1985; Smith and Parker, 1980.
2. Daly and Wilson, 1988; Lundsgaarde, 1977; Wolfgang and Ferracuti, 1967.
3. Mulvihill, Tumin, and Curtis, 1969, cited in Daly and Wilson, 1988, p. 127.
4. Wyatt-Brown, 1982; Ayers, 1984.
5. Bailey, 1989.
6. Nisbett, Polly, and Lang, 1995.
7. Fox and Pierce, 1987.
8. Gastil, 1971.
9. Hackney, 1969.

10. Regression is a statistical technique in which a "dependent" variable such as life satisfaction is examined in relation to a number of "independent" (predictor) variables, for example, income, education, and age. The resulting analysis gives a "regression co-efficient" for each predictor variable. This coefficient, similar to a correlation coefficient, is an index of the degree to which the predictor variable is related to the dependent variable, controlling for the effects of the other predictor variables.

11. Some studies examine entire states (Baron and Straus, 1988; Gastil, 1971; Huff-Corzine, Corzine, and Moore, 1986; Loftin and Hill, 1974; Parker and Smith, 1979; Smith & Parker, 1980). But of course states differ in many ways that are associated with homicide rate, including percent living in large metropolitan areas (Archer and Gartner, 1984; Friday, 1983; Harries, 1974, 1980; Nettler, 1984; Wolfgang and Ferracuti, 1967), average population density (Galle, Gove, and McPherson, 1972; McPherson, 1972; Schmitt, 1966; Winsborough, 1970), and the nature of the economy and ecology, including factors that are plausibly related to gun ownership, such as percent of the population involved in agrarian activities. Other studies examine cities or Standard Metropolitan Statistical Areas (SMSAs) (Blau and Blau, 1982; Gastil, 1971; Loftin and Parker, 1985; McCarthy, Galle, and Zimmern, 1975; Messner, 1982, 1983; Parker, 1989; Simpson, 1985; Williams, 1984). But when cities or SMSAs are studied, it is only the largest units that are examined, and they are studied in the same "aggregated" analysis, that is, rates for cities of all sizes are included in the dependent variable, as are rates for both blacks and whites. Only two studies distinguish between white and black homicide rates (Harer and Steffensmeier, 1992; Messner and Gordon, 1992), and those do not examine rates for different city sizes separately.

12. Fox and Pierce, 1987.

13. Klein, 1962; Gordon, 1986; Land, McCall, and Cohen, 1990.

14. Data are from the supplementary homicide records of Fox and Pierce, 1987.

15. Data for all 70 central cities larger than 200,000 are reported. The other cities were randomly sampled to select 4 of each size from each state, unless there were 4 or fewer in a given category, in which case all cities of the size were included in the sample. This resulted in a sample of 188 small cities and 141 medium-size cities.

16. When we examined our data at highly aggregated levels, analyzing all city sizes and both black and white data in the same regression analyses, we found the same pattern as found in the literature in general. (The full correlation matrix may be seen in Table A.1 of Appendix A.) We found that southernness is correlated with both male offender rates and victim rates at moderate levels (.40 and .35 respectively), but that poverty and percent black are both better predictors of homicide rates (.73 and .72 for poverty and .79 and .78 for percent black). This reflects precisely the sort of situation in which the effect of southernness is likely to be underestimated by regression analyses. And in fact it is the case that southernness is only a very weak predictor of homicide rates when other variables are controlled for. (Results of these analyses are presented in Table A.2 of Appendix A.) The standardized coefficient for southernness (directly comparable to a correlation coefficient) is only .16 for male offender rates and .13 for victim rates. Contributions of the other variables also duplicate the most frequent patterns of other studies—that is, important contributions made by poverty, population size, and percent black, and weak contributions made by the GINI index of inequality, population density, and percent of males 15–29, as may be seen in Table A.2. Thus our regression analyses reflect the general findings in the literature when highly aggregated data are analyzed.

17. Reaves, 1993; Reaves and Nisbett, 1995.
18. Reed, 1981; Simpson, 1985; Smith and Parker, 1980.
19. Reed, 1981, p. 13.
20. Cohen and Nisbett, 1994.
21. Cohen and Nisbett, 1994.

3

Differences Between Northerners and Southerners in Attitudes Toward Violence

T HE MOST OBVIOUS place to look for cultural differences that might account for southerners' penchant for homicide would be their attitudes toward violence. As it happens, there are a few differences in attitudes toward violence between southerners and northerners that occasionally appear in national polls. The attitudes are those toward spanking children (more favored in the South); gun control (more opposed in the South); and various U.S. military undertakings (more supported in the South). All these are interpretable as differences in attitudes toward violence, but they do not deal with serious interpersonal violence and each could be explained without resort to notions of a culture of honor.

If it is participation in a culture of honor that motivates the greater tendency toward homicide in the South, then it should be possible to show that southerners are more in favor of violence used for answering affronts and for defending themselves. In addition, if violence is appropriate behavior for adults, we would expect that idea to be conveyed to children by socialization agents, through modeling violence and teaching its use in relations with peers.

Note, however, that there is no reason to expect southerners to be more in favor of violence in general than northerners are, just as southerners are no more likely to kill in the context of a felony than northerners are. Members of cultures of honor may be expected to use violence only as a means to achieve certain socially approved ends.

Two major sources of attitude data on violence are in the public domain and available for reanalysis: data collected by the National Opinion Research Center (NORC) over the past two decades and data reported in 1972 by Monica Blumenthal and her colleagues in a classic survey of American attitudes toward violence.[1] We present our reanalyses of their data and add our own survey data.

In the three studies that follow, we present data on white male respondents only. We excluded women from analyses because men are responsible for the vast majority of violent acts and because the culture of honor is interwoven with cultural concepts of masculinity. We excluded people of color because the lack of a regional difference in homicide rates suggests that cultural factors may be different for blacks and whites. Similar points are likely to apply to the very broad and diverse category "Hispanic." When we say "southerners" or "non-southerners," we do not intend to overgeneralize but are merely using the terms as a shorthand way of saying "southern white males" and "nonsouthern white males."[2]

We have several reasons to believe that the results we present below cannot be explained by regional demographic differences in income, education, or age: (1) The analyses controlled for income, education, and age. (2) It makes little difference in results when analyses do not control for these variables, perhaps because white northerners and southerners differ only slightly on those variables. And, perhaps most important, (3) the pattern of responses characteristic of southerners—endorsement of violence limited to use in self-defense, response to insult, and social control—is unique. Age, income, and education all predict some items, but none predicts the same pattern of responses that the region variable does.[3] All the differences between southerners and non-southerners that we report in this chapter, unless otherwise noted, are statistically significant at at least the .05 level by two-tailed tests.

Violence in General Versus Violence for Purposes of Protection

We obtained data from the Blumenthal et al.[4] survey of attitudes of American men toward violence. Sampling and data analysis information for this study can be found in Appendix B.[5]

Violence in General

When questions were asked about violence in the abstract and when questions dealt with specific violence unrelated to honor or self-protection, few differences between the South (defined as census divisions 5, 6, and 7: see bottom-of-page note in Chapter 2) and the Non-South were found. Those differences that were found were as likely to show southerners being *more* opposed to violence than northerners as they were to show the reverse. For example, southerners were more likely to say, "It is sometimes necessary to use violence to prevent violence," but they were also more likely to say, "When a person harms you, you should turn the other cheek and forgive him." On a question that asked respondents which was worse—hurting people or damaging property—southerners were more likely than northerners to say hurting people was worse.

Violence for Defense of Self and Home

On questions concerning self-protection, however, the pattern was very different. It may be seen in Figure 3.1 that southerners were more likely to agree that "a man has the right to kill another man in self-defense," that "a man has the right to kill a person to defend his family," and that "a man has the right to kill a person to defend his house." Answers to the last question are striking when compared to answers to the question about whether it is worse to hurt people or damage property. As a matter of abstract principle, southerners were more likely to see harming people as worse than damaging property; yet when a specific case of protecting one's house was invoked, they were more likely to endorse lethal violence against the perpetrator.

Violence for Social Control

The principle that violence is a legitimate means of self-protection seems extrapolated to the principle that violence is a legitimate means of protecting

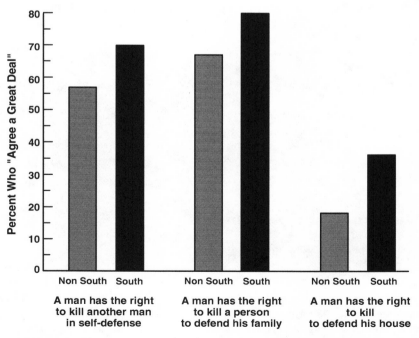

FIGURE 3.1   Percent of southern and nonsouthern respondents agreeing "a great deal" to three different propositions about killing. Source: Cohen and Nisbett, 1994, from Blumenthal et al., 1972.

order and establishing social control more generally. It may be seen in Figure 3.2 that southerners were more likely than nonsoutherners to advocate violence in dealing with: (1) "hoodlums who have gone into a town, terrified people, and caused a lot of property damage"; (2) "student disturbances on campus and elsewhere which involve a lot of property damage"; and (3) "big city riots." With respect to those situations, southerners were less likely to say that police should "let it go" and they were more likely to say that police should either "shoot, but not to kill" or actually "shoot to kill."

Interestingly, though southerners were more likely to endorse violence to protect and restore order, they were not more likely to endorse violence to bring about change. If the results in Figure 3.2 regarding violence for social control were solely the product of greater southern support for the status quo, one might expect southerners to be less approving of violence for social change. However, that was not the case. The Blumenthal survey included fifteen items measuring approval of violence for social change. Differences between the South and Non-South were slight and nonsignificant for fourteen of the fifteen items.

Thus, southerners were not more approving of violence in all forms. Rather, it seems that southerners were more likely than nonsoutherners to see violence as a tool with a special use—to protect self, home, and institutions when those appear threatened.

Responses to Insult

One scenario dealt with violence used to answer an insult. Respondents were told about a policeman who punched a man and knocked him down after the man swore at him and called him a pig. Southerners were more likely than nonsoutherners to say that they or their friends would feel similarly if they were in the officer's shoes. More evidence about violence in response to affronts comes from the General Social Surveys and from work by Cohen and Nisbett described below.[6]

Violence in Response to Insults

Responses to Affronts: General Social Surveys

The General Social Surveys conducted by the National Opinion Research Center are national polls covering a variety of social and political issues. The questions relevant to interpersonal violence all have to do with the appropriateness of punching someone under various circumstances. Again, results are based on analyses for white males and control for income, education, and age. The number of respondents was very large, generally around 2,000 for southerners and 4,000 for nonsoutherners. Sampling information can be found in Appendix B.

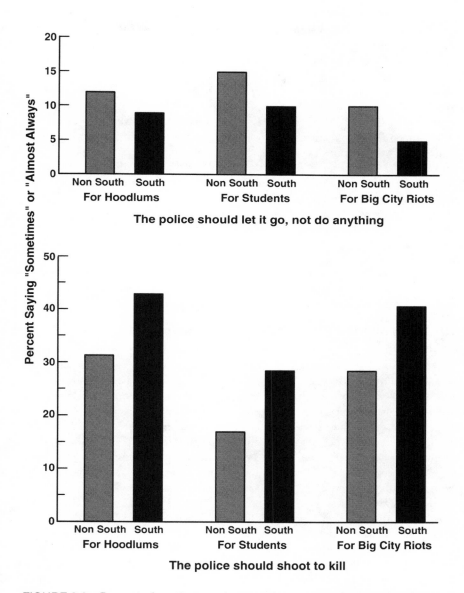

FIGURE 3.2 Percent of southern and nonsouthern respondents stating that police should do nothing, and percent stating that police should shoot to kill, for various disturbances. Source: Cohen and Nisbett, 1994, from Blumenthal et al., 1972.

Southerners (respondents from census divisions 5, 6, and 7) were very slightly more likely than nonsoutherners to endorse the notion that it could sometimes be right for "a man to punch an adult male stranger" or for "a policeman to strike an adult male citizen." Raw mean difference for each item was 2 percent—significant because of the huge number of respondents and because controlling for demographic variables slightly amplified the effect of region. In specific scenarios, however, southerners were more likely than nonsoutherners to endorse a man's hitting another person only if that person's behavior could be construed as an affront—if the person were in a protest march expressing opposition to the man's views, or if the person were drunk and bumped into the man and his wife on the street, or if the person had hit the man's child. Southerners were also more likely to approve of a policeman's hitting a citizen who had said vulgar and obscene things to him.[7]

Southerners were not more likely to endorse violence for specific situations not involving insults. That is, they were not more likely to approve of a man's hitting another person if that person "was beating up a woman," "was being questioned as a suspect in a murder case," or "was attempting to escape from custody." The lack of difference on the question concerning "beating up a woman" provides a useful control because it clearly involves the issue of protection—just not protection of one's self or one's own family.

Responses to Affronts: Survey of Rural Counties

To establish more firmly that the South has a version of the culture of honor, we conducted our own survey of counties in the rural South and Midwest. We compared rural areas because of the assumption, based in part on our empirical findings on homicide rates, that the culture of the Old South would be preserved best in rural areas.

Southern respondents were from census divisions 5, 6, and 7—South Atlantic, East South Central, West South Central—the same as in the national studies. Midwestern respondents came from census division 4—Minnesota, Iowa, Missouri, North Dakota, South Dakota, Nebraska, and Kansas. This region, representing the heartland Midwest, seemed more ecologically and economically similar to the South than any other non-South region. Both division 4 and the South are characterized by low population densities and substantially agricultural economies. Sampling information is in Appendix B.

The mean age was 50 for both the 144 midwestern respondents and the 125 southern respondents. The mean family income was $43,342 in the Midwest and $42,232 in the South. The mean years of education were 12.73 in the Midwest and 12.46 in the South. None of these differences is at all close to significance. The similarity of the two samples is not due to matching or any other departure from random sampling procedure. It thus seems likely that whites in those southern rural counties are little different from whites in that set of midwestern rural counties with respect to those important demographic variables.

That fact is particularly helpful because it makes it implausible that demographic differences could account for regional differences. (In our analyses, we controlled for income, education, and age to make doubly sure of that and to increase the power of our statistical tests.)

We gave respondents a series of vignettes involving affront or protection issues. For three of the items, we told respondents about a man named Fred and asked how justified Fred would be in fighting an acquaintance who had affronted him in some way. We asked how justified it would be if Fred fights an acquaintance because that person "looks over Fred's girlfriend and starts talking to her in a suggestive way," "insults Fred's wife, implying that she has loose morals," or "tells others behind Fred's back that Fred is a liar and a cheat." On two more items, we told respondents about more serious affronts and asked how justified Fred would be in *shooting* the person who had committed the action. We asked how justified it would be if Fred shoots another because that person "sexually assaults Fred's 16-year-old daughter" or "steals Fred's wife." On follow-up questions for each item, subjects were asked whether, if Fred failed to take violent action, they would think he was "not much of a man."

It may be seen in Figure 3.3 that southern respondents, on average, were more likely to see strong justification for Fred's taking violent action. The difference was particularly dramatic on the sexual assault of the daughter question, with 47 percent of southerners saying the shooting would be "extremely justified," compared to only 26 percent of northerners. On the follow-up questions, more southerners gave answers consistent with a masculine ethic demanding violence in defense of honor, self, and family. Across the five questions, they were more likely than midwesterners to say Fred would be "not much of a man" if he did not respond violently. Again, the sexual assault question showed particularly strong differences, with 23 percent of southern respondents thinking Fred would be "not much of a man" if he didn't shoot the person who assaulted his daughter, compared to only 10 percent of midwestern respondents.

Fighting to answer an affront is part of the masculine ideal for southerners in a way that it is not for midwesterners. We asked respondents to give their judgments of a man who fights if "deeply insulted by an acquaintance." Respondents could say the man "fits well" or "fits poorly" their definition of manhood; as predicted, midwesterners were more likely than southerners to say this man "fits poorly" their definition of being a man (52 percent versus 37 percent). This difference was not due simply to midwesterners' being more nonviolent generally. When questions were asked about men who fight when there has been no affront, midwesterners and southerners gave the same assessment of the men.

Another item captured the importance of honor for interpersonal relations in the South. We asked respondents how long their friendship would be disrupted if a friend of theirs (1) got into a fist fight with them over a game of some kind or (2) called them a liar and a coward during an argument over a bet. As may be

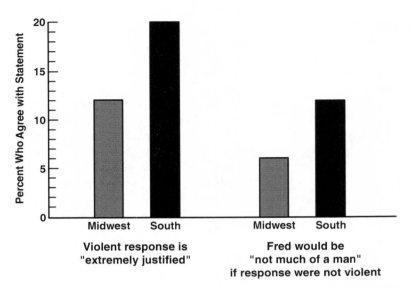

FIGURE 3.3   Percent of southerners and midwesterners saying a violent response to various scenarios is "extremely justified" and that protagonist would be
"not much of a man" if he did not respond violently. Source: Cohen and Nisbett,

seen in Figure 3.4, midwesterners saw the two events as equally disruptive to
the friendships, whereas southerners saw the insult as much more harmful.

We also asked several questions from the General Social Survey about approval of punching a stranger. Our results were comparable to those of NORC
in direction and magnitude for the "protest march" item and the item about the
"drunk who bumps into a man and his wife." The results for the bumping question for both our survey and the NORC survey are shown in Figure 3.5. (Unlike NORC, we found no difference for the item in which someone says vulgar
and obscene things to the policeman.) The remaining three items were not related to honor or self-protection, so we did not expect southerners to be significantly more violent on these questions; and in fact, they were not.

Socialization for Violence

The data from the three surveys suggest that southerners are more likely than
nonsoutherners to view violence as a legitimate response to insult, as an appropriate means of self-protection, and as a justifiable tool for restoring order.
Inasmuch as children can scarcely be expected to carry out violence without
proper preparation for it, we would expect these lessons to be taught to children in the process of socialization. There is substantial evidence that, across

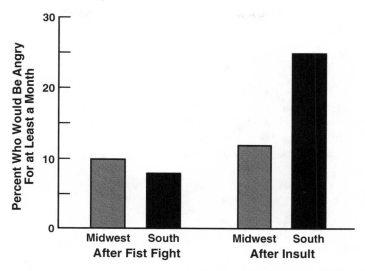

FIGURE 3.4   Percent of southerners and midwesterners saying they would be angry with a friend for at least a month following a fist fight and following an insult. Source: Cohen and Nisbett, 1994.

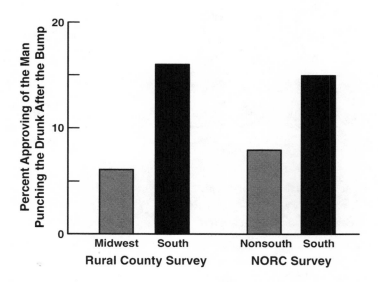

FIGURE 3.5   Percent of southerners and midwesterners who approved punching "a drunk who bumps into a man and his wife." Sources: Cohen and Nisbett, 1994; Davis and Smith, 1990.

cultures, there is an association between harsh socialization and incidence of violence among adults.[8]

We found southerners to be more likely to endorse violence for disciplining children. It may be seen in Figure 3.6 that southerners, when asked a general question taken from NORC about whether spanking is sometimes necessary to discipline a child, were more likely to advocate it. In both our sample and the NORC General Social Survey sample, a substantially higher fraction of southerners agreed that a "good, hard spanking" was sometimes necessary. For a specific infraction like shoplifting from the local grocery store, a substantial majority of southerners endorsed spanking their child, whereas slightly less than half the midwesterners did so.

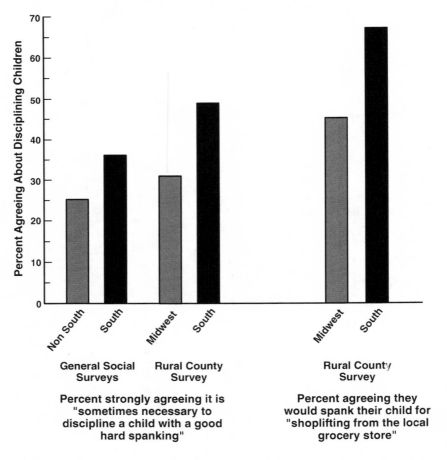

FIGURE 3.6   Percent of southerners and midwesterners agreeing with propositions about spanking children. Source: Cohen and Nisbett, 1994.

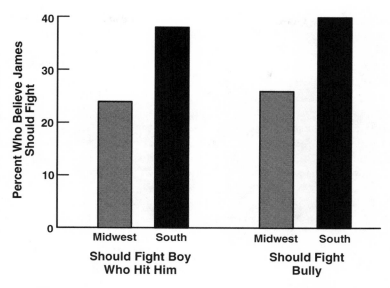

FIGURE 3.7   Percent of southerners and midwesterners believing a boy should fight after being hit or bullied for his lunch money. Source: Cohen and Nisbett, 1994.

We also asked respondents what they thought most fathers would expect their 10-year-old son to do in two situations. In the first situation, a boy named James was beaten up by another boy in front of a crowd of children. In the second situation, James was repeatedly bullied by another boy who stole his lunch money. As may be seen in Figure 3.7, in both cases, southerners were more likely than midwesterners to say that James would be expected to "take a stand and fight the other boy."

Survey Data on Guns and Gun Control

Because of southerners' stronger ethic of self-protection, we would expect them to be more likely to possess tools often used for that purpose—namely, guns. National surveys invariably show that southerners are indeed more likely to own guns. But surveys also show that the differences go beyond mere gun ownership. Not only are southerners more likely to own guns; they are more likely to see their guns as instruments of protection (as opposed to purely for sport), more likely to carry their guns with them, more likely to feel safe if they have a gun around the house, and more ready to use their guns if their homes are broken into.

Gun ownership rates were relatively high in our own survey of rural areas and did not differ by region. Our survey showed no difference in pistol, rifle, shotgun, or overall gun ownership. However, there was a great difference when respondents were asked whether their gun was used for sport or for protection. Only 21 percent of midwestern gun owners said the gun was used at least partly for protection, whereas 49 percent of southern gun owners said the gun was used at least partly for protection.

Other surveys also illustrate that southerners are more likely to keep a gun around for self-defense purposes. In 1981, a Gallup poll asked respondents about twelve different "things people do because of their concern over crime." In response to this concern, southerners were more likely to say they carried a weapon and that they had bought a gun, as may be seen in Figure 3.8. In contrast, they did not report taking more "peaceable" preventive measures, for example, carrying a whistle, keeping lights on at night, or locking doors.

In 1976, the National Election Study asked a similar question.[9] Southern white males were almost twice as likely as nonsouthern white males to say they "kept a gun for purposes of protection." Again, it was not that southerners were more concerned about crime generally. Respondents were also asked about four nonviolent preventive measures, including keeping a dog for purposes of protection, putting new locks on windows or doors, putting an alarm system in the car, home, or apartment, and staying away from certain areas in a town or

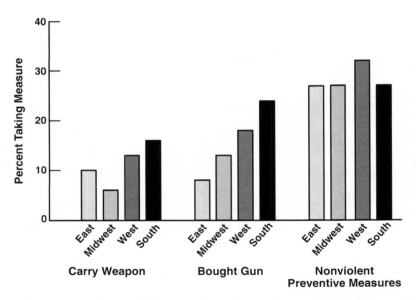

FIGURE 3.8   Percent of respondents in different regions of the country taking various measures against crime. Source: Gallup, 1981, pp. 12–13.

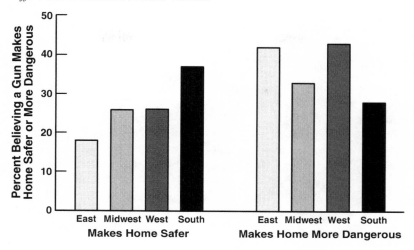

FIGURE 3.9 Percent of respondents in different regions of the country who believe having a gun in the home makes it safer or more dangerous. Source: Flanigan and Jamieson, 1986.

city. If anything, southerners were less likely to take nonviolent preventive measures than nonsoutherners.

Polls conducted in 1984 and 1986 by Media General/Associated Press also showed that guns were more available and ready for use in the South.[10] The 1984 polls showed that southerners were much more likely to keep a gun at home (55 percent versus less than 40 percent for the rest of the country) and to carry a gun or other weapon to protect themselves (15 percent versus less than 8 percent for the rest of the country). Respondents were also asked whether they felt a home was safer with or without a gun in it. As may be seen in Figure 3.9, the South was the only region where the modal answer was that a gun made the home a safer place. Perhaps because southerners view their guns as so essential to self-protection, they are more reluctant to have guns controlled by the government. This is shown in numerous Gallup polls and in NORC and National Election Study data.

The Southern Ideology of Violence

The South seems to have a different ideology about violence than the rest of the country has. The data of Blumenthal et al. showed that southerners were not more in favor of violence in general, that they were not more in favor of violence in many specified contexts unrelated to culture-of-honor concerns, but that they were more likely to endorse violence when it was used for self-protection and for social control. The NORC and our rural county data also showed that southerners were no more likely to endorse violence than northerners in a wide variety of specific situations. It was only for situations involving an affront, the protection of self, home, or family, and the socialization of children that southerners were more likely to endorse violence. Thus, southern ideology does not make all violence acceptable but, rather, allows violence as a tool for special purposes.

The differences in ideology by no means simply reflect structural or demographic differences between the South and other regions. Differences between regions remain—in fact are typically greater—when age, education, and income are taken into account, and these variables predict a different pattern of responses than the region variable does.

The lawless frontier moved further south and further west with every decade from the beginning of the seventeenth century to the end of the nineteenth. The herding economy in its various forms moved with it. In the South, the frontier is now gone and few people continue to earn their living by herding. But it appears that the violence and ideology toward violence created by these conditions have persevered.

The regional differences in attitudes provide a plausible explanation for the regional differences in homicide. The culture of honor, the self-protection ethic, and the widespread presence of guns may reinforce each other in a dynamic way. To spell out the cycle: In a culture where honor is so important, arguments lead to affronts that demand retribution. The availability of guns increases the chance that the retribution may be deadly. In addition, the knowledge that the other person may be armed and may begin acting violently may lead to preemptive first strikes. Once conflicts escalate, a man may be more apt to take a first strike as a matter of self-protection before he himself gets shot. At a cultural level, the occurrence of hundreds of these violent self-fulfilling prophecies creates a milieu where the threat of violence keeps individuals vigilant (perhaps hypervigilant) in their own defense.

Passion killings that began as arguments, lovers' quarrels, family disputes, and the like are what elevate southern homicide rates today.[11] And it is easy to see why these events are so dangerous in the southern context of concern with personal honor. In such a milieu, there are high costs for backing down from a challenge, *and everyone knows it.* Once the gauntlet has been thrown down, the preemptive first strike may be construed by some as a necessary act of self-defense.

Perhaps that is also why southerners have a reputation for being so polite. The best way to keep a conflict from spiraling out of hand is to avoid the conflict in the first place. So southern hospitality, politeness, and friendliness are what keep social interactions going smoothly. As Robert Heinlein noted, "An armed society is a polite society."[12]

A telling passage from Grady McWhiney's book on southern culture shows how issues of honor, protection, the ready availability of guns, and the social approval of violence were tied together in the Old South.

As an observer in the South noted, enemies would meet, exchange insults, and one would shoot the other down, professing that he had acted in self-defense because he believed the victim was armed. When such a story was told in court, "in a community where it is not a strange thing for men to carry about their persons deadly weapons, [each member of the jury] feels that he would have done the same thing under similar circumstances so that in condemning him they would but condemn themselves." Consequently, they free the slayer, "and a hundred others, our sons and half grown lads amongst them, resolve in their hearts, that since every man may go armed and everyone is therefore justifiable in slaying his enemy, they will do likewise."[13]

It is possible that this passage characterizes some of the violence of the contemporary South as well. But is honor such an important issue in the South today? Southerners do express more concern about insults than do nonsoutherners, but social psychologists know that real behavior is not always readily predictable from expressed attitudes. Do young southern white men today really care about insults? Is their masculinity really put on the line when they are affronted, as survey results would imply? And are they truly prepared to take steps to restore the balance after someone offends them? In Chapter 4 we report on explorations of these questions in a laboratory setting.

Notes

1. Davis and Smith, 1990; and Blumenthal, Kahn, Andrews, and Head, 1972.
2. Our reanalyses of national surveys include all questions we could find concerning endorsements of interpersonal violence. In analyzing our own data and data from other surveys, we used continuous-level variables, and we report significance levels based on continuous-variable analyses that controlled for income, education, and age. However, for ease of understanding and comparing the magnitude of differences across questions, we present all results in raw percentage form.
3. The pattern of responses predicted by age, education, and income is discussed more extensively in Cohen and Nisbett, 1994.
4. Blumenthal et al., 1972.
5. Complete details about this study and others in this chapter can be found in Cohen and Nisbett, 1994.
6. Cohen and Nisbett, 1994.
7. Again, complete presentation of the results can be found in Cohen and Nisbett, 1994. Results of the drunk-bumping-into-the-man question—both for the NORC survey and our rural county survey—can be seen in Figure 3.5.
8. Ross 1985, 1986, cited in Knauft, 1991.

9. Center for Political Studies, 1979.

10. Cited in Flanagan and Jamieson, 1988; Flanagan and McGarrell, 1986.

11. Reed, 1981; Nisbett, 1993.

12. Cited in Will, 1993, p. 93

13. McWhiney, 1988, p. 163; quotations from J. A. Lyon in *Columbus Eagle* (Columbus, Miss.), June 1, 1855.

4

Insult, Anger, and Aggression: An "Experimental Ethnography" of the Culture of Honor

WE HAVE ARGUED FROM the anecdotal and historical data in Chapter 1, the archival homicide data in Chapter 2, and the survey data in Chapter 3 that southerners, because they belong to a culture in which insults are a very serious matter, are more violent than nonsoutherners. Insults cannot be ignored, because a man's reputation for strength and toughness is compromised until he proves himself through violence, or at least through dominant or aggressive behavior signaling a capacity for violence.

We still need to show, however, that behaviors and attitudes are linked in the way our theory specifies. The relation between attitudes and behavior is often not straightforward: People sometimes merely pay lip service to attitudes without behaving in ways consistent with them, or sometimes they earnestly hold such attitudes but never manage to find ways to act them out. In any case, decades of research by social psychologists have shown that there can be large gaps between expressed attitudes and actual behavior. Measures of behavior are needed before one can take seriously hypotheses about cultural difference.

In the experiments reported here, which we conducted with Brian Bowdle and Norbert Schwarz,[1] we examined the sequence of reactions following an insult, in an effort to determine whether southerners become more upset by affronts and are more likely to take aggressive action to compensate for the diminishment they experience. We brought southerners and northerners into the lab, where an associate of the experimenter, who did not appear to be part of the study, rudely insulted them. We observed subjects' emotional reactions, physiological responses, and actions in response to this insult.

When we refer to northerners and southerners who participated in the experiments, we use those words as a shorthand way of referring to male students from the North and the South attending the University of Michigan who are white, non-Hispanic, and non-Jewish. Our sample is certainly not a representative one—even of white non-Hispanic, non-Jewish males. The students came from families that were financially well-off on average, with the median income for northerners being about $85,000 and for southerners, $95,000. The southerners might also be unusual in that they chose to leave the South at least temporarily and come to school in the North. We suspect both of these factors worked to mute regional differences and that regional effects would be bigger if more-representative samples of northerners and southerners were drawn. Southern and northern students differed from each other in remarkably few respects other than region of origin. Southerners were defined, as in Chapters 2, 3, and 5, as individuals from census divisions 5, 6, and 7, though the definition had to be broadened slightly in Experiments 2 and 3 to increase the number of eligible southerners. (Details about subject characteristics are found in Appendix C.)

Experiment 1: Cognitive and Emotional Reactions to an Insult

The three experiments all took place in the laboratory of the Institute for Social Research at the University of Michigan. All three explored consequences of the same basic situation: A confederate of the experimenter bumped into the unsuspecting subject as he walked down a hallway and called him an "asshole."

Procedure

In Experiment 1, we examined the effect of this insult on the immediate emotional reaction of the subject and on hostility expressed at a later point in the experiment. Subsequent hostility was assessed with a word-completion task and a face-rating task. Hostility was also assessed by having the subject complete two scenarios: one neutral and one that involved affront and sexual challenge. These procedures allowed us to examine whether the subject would project his anger onto ambiguous, neutral stimuli after the insult or whether only stimuli that involved affront and challenge would bring out southerners' aggression after the insult.

Forty-two northern and forty-one southern students came to the laboratory, where they were told they would be participating in a study concerning the effect of response-time constraints on judgment. After an initial introduction to the study, subjects were asked to fill out a brief demographic questionnaire and take it to a table at the end of a long, narrow hallway.

As the subject walked down the hall, a confederate of the experimenter walked out of a door marked "Photo Lab" and began working at a file cabinet in the hall. The confederate had to push the file drawer in to allow the subject to pass by him and drop his paper off at the table. As the subject returned seconds later and walked back down the hall toward the experimental room, the confederate (who had just reopened the file drawer) slammed it shut on seeing the subject approach, bumped into him with his shoulder, and called the subject an "asshole." The confederate then walked back into the "Photo Lab."

Two observers were stationed in the hall. They appeared to be working on homework, paying no attention to the goings-on in the hall. One observer, a male, was seated on the floor in a location where he could glance up and see the subject's face at the moment he was bumped. The other observer, a female, was sitting at the table at the end of the hall where she could glance at the subject's face if he turned around (which occurred about 86 percent of the time). Both observers could hear everything the subject said and could read his body language (though from different perspectives). Immediately after the bumping incident, the observers rated the subject's emotional reactions on seven-point scales.[2] Of course, observers did not know the regional origin of the subject. Subjects assigned to the control condition dropped their questionnaires off but were not bumped and no one was present in the hall.

Neutral Stimuli. After the subject returned to the room, the judgment tasks began. The first three tasks had relatively neutral content. They were studied in order to examine whether southerners would "project" hostility onto neutral stimuli after an affront. The first task was a word completion task, in which the subject was given a string of letters (for example, _ight or gu_) that he could complete in either a hostile way (fight or gun) or a nonhostile way (light or gum). The second task was a face-rating task, in which the subject tried to guess what emotion was being expressed in a series of photographs of faces— anger, fear, disgust, sadness, or happiness. The third task was a scenario completion task, in which the subject needed to fill in the beginning or ending of a story. In the neutral scenario, a man was rescued by an ambulance and the subject was asked to fill in the beginning of the story.

Insult Prime Scenario. Another scenario presented a clear affront, however. The scenario began:

It had only been about twenty minutes since they had arrived at the party when Jill pulled Steve aside, obviously bothered about something.

"What's wrong?" asked Steve.

"It's Larry. I mean, he knows that you and I are engaged, but he's already made two passes at me tonight."

Jill walked back into the crowd, and Steve decided to keep his eye on Larry. Sure enough, within five minutes Larry was reaching over and trying to kiss Jill.

Subjects were asked to complete the ending to this story.

After all tasks were completed, subjects were thoroughly debriefed and reconciled with the "bumper."[3]

Results

Emotional reactions.   Northerners and southerners differed in how angry or amused they appeared to be after the bump. Observers rated southern subjects as significantly less amused by the bump than northern subjects[4] and marginally more angry than northern subjects.[5] We subtracted the amusement rating from the anger rating for each subject to show the very different reaction patterns of northerners and southerners. As may be seen in Figure 4.1, the most common emotional reaction for northerners was to show more amusement than anger. The overwhelmingly dominant reaction for southerners was to show as much or more anger than amusement.[6]

Projective Hostility for Neutral Stimuli.   We examined whether the insult would make southerners more hostile even to neutral stimuli but leave northerners unaffected. There was no such pattern for any of the word completion, face rating, or neutral scenario completion tasks. Neither northerners nor southerners were much affected by the insult, and northerners did not differ from southerners overall.

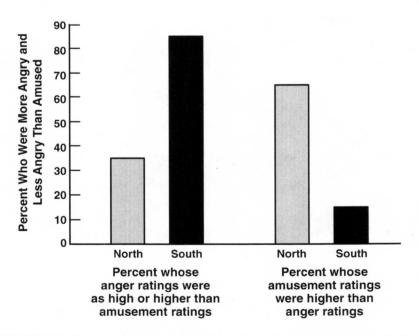

FIGURE 4.1   Pattern of emotional reactions of southern and northern subjects to insult

Hostility in Response to Insult Prime Scenario. For the scenario describing the attempted pass at the fiancée, the insult had very different consequences for northerners and southerners. If southerners were insulted, they were much more likely to end this scenario with violence; northerners were unaffected by the insult. Fully 75 percent of insulted southerners completed this scenario with events in which the man injured or threatened to injure his challenger, whereas only 20 percent of noninsulted southerners did so.[7] Northerners were unaffected by the manipulation, actually being trivially less likely to conclude this scenario with violence if they had been insulted than if they had not (41 percent versus 55 percent).[8]

In sum, southerners, unlike northerners, were likely to see the insult as a cause for anger rather than amusement, and they were much more likely to complete the "affront" script with violence if they had been insulted than if they had not. Interestingly, insulted southerners were no more likely to project hostility onto neutral stimuli than other subjects. These findings indicate that an insult may make a southerner angry and—although it does not produce hostility in response to innocuous stimuli—the insult does lower his threshold for angry thoughts in response to subsequent affronts.

Experiment 2:
Physiological Reactions to an Insult

In Experiment 2, we explored whether southerners' responses to the insult went beyond expressions of annoyance and mere "cognitive" priming for aggression, and examined whether they were accompanied by physiological changes of a sort that might mediate real behavioral aggression.

Procedure

Physiological Measure of Stress. To measure how upset or stressed the subject became, we examined the cortisol level of the subject before and after the bump. Cortisol is a hormone associated with high levels of stress, anxiety, and arousal in humans and in animals.[9] If southerners are more upset by the acute stress of the insult, they should show a rise in cortisol levels compared to control subjects. If northerners are relatively unaffected by the insult, as they seemed to be in Experiment 1, they should show little or no rise in cortisol levels compared to control subjects. To measure this, we obtained saliva samples allowing for assays of cortisol levels before and after the bump.

Physiological Measure of Preparedness for Future Aggression. To measure how prepared for future challenges subjects became, we examined their testosterone levels. Testosterone is a hormone associated with aggression and dominance behavior in animals and humans. The causation seems to go both ways: High levels of testosterone facilitate dominance or aggressive behaviors, and successful dominance encounters lead to increases in testosterone.[10] Research suggests that testosterone plays a role in preparing participants for competitions or dominance contests,[11] perhaps by facilitating the aggressive behaviors and display of dominance cues that make one act and even look tougher. In addition, testosterone may raise fear thresholds. In male rats, injections of testosterone act as an "anxiolytic" agent, reducing the rats' fear of novel environments.[12] It would obviously be useful in challenge or competition situations if this fear-reducing effect were to occur in humans. Testosterone levels were also measured by assay of saliva sample.

If southerners respond to the insult as a challenge and are preparing themselves for future aggression or dominance contests, we would expect a testosterone increase after the bump. If northerners are relatively unaffected, we would not expect their testosterone levels to rise very much.

Sequence of Events.   The 111 northern students and 62 southern students were met in the laboratory by an experimenter who explained that the study concerned people's performance on tasks under various conditions. The experimenter said that she would be measuring the subject's blood sugar levels throughout the experiment by taking saliva samples. To get a baseline measurement, the subject was given a piece of sugarless gum to generate saliva, a test tube to fill to the 5 ml level, and a brief questionnaire to fill out as he provided the first sample.

After the saliva sample was given, the subject was sent down the hall to drop off his questionnaire and was bumped and insulted as described in Experiment 1. The subject was bumped publicly, bumped privately, or not bumped at all. In the public condition, there were two male witnesses to the insult. Both witnesses were confederates of the experimenter, but had been identified as fellow subjects by the experimenter before the subject began his walk down the hall. Both observers made eye contact with the subject so that the subject knew they had witnessed the incident. In the private condition, there were no observers in the hallway. And in the control condition, the subject was not bumped or insulted.[13]

After a few minutes, the subject and two confederates were called to the experimental room (in the public condition, the confederates were the same two men who had seen the subject get insulted). The experimenter explained that the subjects would be performing mechanical aptitude tasks and she asked them to give another saliva sample. On average, this second sample was given thirteen minutes after the first. The experimenter then asked the subject to fill out an "opinions test." This questionnaire had a number of scenarios that were ambiguous with respect to whether an insult had been delivered. In one scenario, for example, one character cuts another off as they are driving down the road. For each situation, the subject was asked to guess the likelihood of a physical fight or a verbal argument occurring. After the subject finished the questionnaire, he was asked to give another saliva sample. On average, this third sample was given twenty-five minutes after the first.[14]

Results

We anticipated that publicly insulted subjects would show a more extreme pattern of responses than privately insulted subjects. However, that did not happen, so we combined publicly and privately insulted subjects into one insult condition.

Cortisol Levels. We averaged the two post-bump measurements and then computed a change score: (average post-bump cortisol level minus pre-bump cortisol level) divided by (pre-bump cortisol level). As may be seen in Figure 4.2, cortisol levels rose 79 percent for insulted southerners and 42 percent for control southerners. The levels rose 33 percent for insulted northerners and 39 percent for control northerners. Thus, as anticipated, insulted southerners showed large increases in cortisol level, whereas control southerners and both insulted and control northerners showed much smaller changes.[15]

Testosterone Levels. As with cortisol, we averaged the two post-bump measurements and then computed a change score. As may also be seen in Figure 4.2, testosterone levels rose 12 percent for insulted southerners and 4 percent for control southerners. They rose 6 percent for insulted northerners and

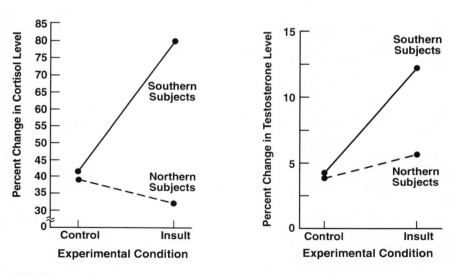

FIGURE 4.2   Change in cortisol levels and change in testosterone levels for insulted and noninsulted southerners and northerners

4 percent for control northerners. As predicted, the change was greater for in-sulted southerners than for subjects in all other conditions.[16]

Ambiguous Insult Scenarios.   Southerners, whether insulted or not, were no more likely than northerners to expect the ambiguous scenarios to end with either physical or verbal aggression. Consistent with the results of Experiment 1, a clear insult seems to be required to prompt angry or aggressive interpreta-tions on the part of southerners.[17]

Experiment 2 showed that southerners became aroused and more prepared for aggression on the physiological level. Southerners were more stressed by the insult, as shown by the rise in their cortisol levels, and more primed for fu-ture aggression, as indicated by the rise in their testosterone levels. Cortisol and testosterone levels of northerners were hardly affected by the insult. We want to emphasize the importance of these physiological findings. They show that the insult produces effects in the southerner that go far beyond mere cog-nitive changes. Southerners are put into a physiological state that should not merely affect interpretations of subsequently encountered affront but could also be expected to impel aggressive action. We explored in Experiment 3 whether such behavioral effects can be demonstrated.

Experiment 3:
Behavioral Reactions to an Insult

In Experiment 3, we tried to extend the results of Experiments 1 and 2 by ex-ploring whether southerners, in accord with a culture-of-honor worldview, would perceive the insult as damaging to their status and reputation and would consequently behave in more aggressive and domineering ways.

Procedure

Subjects were again brought in, given a cover story, and sent down the hall to be bumped or not. After the subject was bumped publicly or privately or not bumped, he continued walking down the long hallway. Another confederate—who was 6 feet 3 inches tall (1.91 meters), weighed 250 pounds (114 kilo-grams), and played college football—appeared around the corner and began walking toward the subject at a good pace. The hall was lined with tables, so there was room for only one person to pass without the other person giving way. The confederate walked determinedly down the center of the hall on a collision course with the subject and did not move (except at the last second to avoid another bumping).

In essence, we set up a "chicken game" similar to that played by American teenagers who drive at each other in their cars (or Albanian shepherds who consider it a dishonor to yield to another person on a narrow mountain path). The confederate estimated the distance at which the subject decided to "chicken out" or give way to him. We expected insulted southern subjects to respond aggressively to the challenge, that is, to go farthest toward the confederate before swerving to avoid a collision.

After playing the chicken game, the subject returned to the experimental room, where he was told that the experiment concerned "who you are" and that "one big part of who we are is who other people think we are." The experimenter explained the importance of first impressions for this and said that sometimes people are aware of the first impressions they make and sometimes they are not. She told the subject that he would have a brief meeting with another subject (actually another confederate, whom we will refer to as the "evaluator"). And she added that the subject's task would be to guess what this other person really thought of him. The subject and his counterpart would be allowed to shake hands, but that was all; no talking was allowed.

The experimenter then brought in the "evaluator" confederate, who shook hands with the subject. In the public bump condition, the evaluator was one of the witnesses to the bump. (In the private bump condition, the evaluator was not one of the observers, and in the control condition, there had been no bump to observe.)

After the brief handshake between the subject and evaluator, the experimenter sent the evaluator out into the hall to record his impressions. The evaluator rated the firmness of the subject's handshake, and he made summary ratings of how domineering or submissive the subject was during the encounter, all on seven-point scales. We expected insulted southern subjects to be more domineering and less submissive after the insult; northerners should be little affected by the insult.

Back in the experimental room, the experimenter explained that the subject would now have to guess what the evaluator thought of him. On a one to five scale, the subject guessed what the other person thought of him on dimensions like "Cowardly-Courageous," "Strong-Weak," "Manly–Not manly" as well as filler dimensions like "Introverted-Extroverted," "Attractive-Unattractive," and so on. Finally, after the subject estimated what the evaluator thought of him, the experimenter asked the subject to rate himself on these dimensions as he really was.

The subject completed another demographic questionnaire and then was debriefed and reconciled with the bumper. Once again, the public versus private nature of the insult was not an important factor in subjects' responses, and we combined the public and private data for analysis.

Results

"Chicken Game."   As may be seen in Figure 4.3 the insult produced aggressive behavior in southerners in the "chicken game." Insulted southerners went much farther before "chickening out" and deferring to the confederate (at about three feet), compared to control southerners (at about nine feet). The insult did not much affect the behavior of northerners.[18]

Encounter with the Evaluator.   As may be seen in Figure 4.3, the insult made southerners less deferential and more domineering. Southern subjects who had been insulted gave firmer handshakes than that those who had not. Northerners were unaffected by the insult.[19]

The overall evaluator rating for how domineering versus submissive the subject was during the encounter showed similar patterns. As may also be seen in Figure 4.3, insulted southerners were rated as much more domineering than control southerners. Northerners were little affected by the insult.[20] Although dominance-related ratings showed the predicted effects, ratings for northerners and southerners were not differentially affected by the insult for items that did not concern dominance or submission (for example, friendliness).

Damage to Masculine Reputation.   Southern and northern control condition subjects, southerners and northerners who had been privately insulted, and northerners who had been insulted in the presence of the evaluator believed they had about equal status in the eyes of the evaluator on dimensions of masculinity. However, as may be seen in Figure 4.4, southerners who had been insulted in the presence of the evaluator believed that their masculine status was damaged in his eyes. That is, they believed the evaluator saw them as less courageous, less manly, more wimpy, and so on.[21]

The Future of an Insult

The findings of these experiments bridge the gap between the survey data showing that southerners are more accepting of violence in response to an insult and the archival data showing that homicide rates are higher in the South. An insult is evidently a very serious matter for southerners. Indeed, the particular insult in these experiments produced a completely different pattern of reactions for southerners than for northerners.

1. Insulted southerners believed that the insult damaged their appearance of strength and masculinity in the eyes of another.
2. Insulted southerners were made more upset by the insult, as indicated by their rise in cortisol levels and the pattern of emotional responses they displayed as rated by observers.
3. Insulted southerners became more cognitively primed for future aggression in insult situations, as indicated by their violent completions of the "attempted kiss script" in Experiment 1.
4. Insulted southerners showed physiological preparedness for dominant and aggressive behaviors, as indicated by their rise in testosterone levels.
5. Insulted southerners behaved in more domineering ways during interpersonal encounters, as shown in the meeting with the evaluator.
6. Insulted southerners actually behaved in physically aggressive ways in subsequent challenge situations, as shown in the "chicken game."

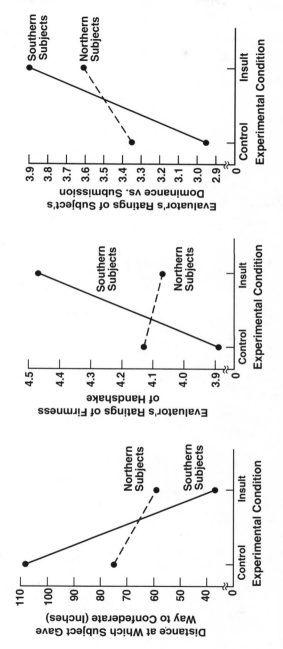

FIGURE 4.3 Distance at which the subject gave way to the confederate in the "chicken game," firmness of handshake, and general domineering versus submissive impression for insulted and noninsulted southerners and northerners

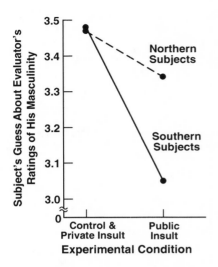

FIGURE 4.4   Perceived masculine status of insulted and noninsulted southerners and northerners

We would never have predicted differences so strong as we found with this college student population. One way to understand the results is to propose that an insult simply has a fundamentally different meaning for northerners and southerners: For the southerner, the insult has something to do with himself and his reputation; for the northerner, the insult has something to do only with the person who delivered the insult.

If the reactions of our subjects bear any similarity to the way southerners react to a real insult in their lives, it is easy to understand why violence in response to an insult is more common in the South than in the North. It is not just that southerners have attitudes that are more approving of violence to answer an insult *in the abstract*. The insulted southerner feels his reputation threatened, he becomes angry, and he is cognitively and physiologically prepared for aggression. The insult is a matter about which something must be done, and aggressive or domineering behavior toward offenders (or even bystanders) is required.

Of course, our laboratory experiments did not produce any truly violent behavior in our subjects, so it is an extrapolation to say that we have shown the process by which an insult results in actual violence for members of a culture of honor. However, we believe it takes more faith to believe that processes such as those shown here would fail to have consequences than to believe the opposite. Anger, arousal, and threat to status clearly constitute an explosive combination that instigates many acts of violence.

People in a culture of honor who respond with aggressive and dominant behaviors after an insult may be acting quite rationally if they are trying to avoid the stigma of the insult from their peers. Recall that in Chapter 3 rural residents of the South were shown to be more likely than those of the North to believe that a man who failed to fight or shoot when presented with affronts was "not much of a man." Similarly, interviews with our subjects showed that many southerners were convinced that it was sometimes necessary to resort to violence in order to show that one is not a "wimp."

We should add that one aspect of our experimental results is puzzling and requires some commentary. The manipulation of the private versus public nature of the insult had little effect. This is somewhat problematic, since the presumed reason that members of a culture of honor find an insult so upsetting is that it lowers one's reputation for being able to defend oneself. If the insult occurs in public, reputation is at stake to a much greater degree.

In retrospect, however, it is not clear that our manipulation was a very good one. The "public" manipulation occurred in front of people the subject had never seen and likely would never see again. Reputation could not be much damaged under those circumstances. A better manipulation would involve insulting subjects in front of acquaintances or friends with whom they expect to interact in the future. The point is important to clarify because it is highly relevant to the theory about the meaning of an insult and the utility of various responses to it.

Until more research is done, however, we may say that the experimental data—added to the homicide rate and attitude data—offer support for three important points: (1) The insult is a much more serious matter to the southerner than to the northerner. (2) It is more serious because an insult makes the affronted southerner feel diminished. (3) Consequently the affronted southerner may use aggressive or domineering behavior to reestablish his masculine status.

In Chapter 5 we turn from individual psychology to more public representations—asking whether laws, public policies, and institutions reflect and encourage the kind of individual attitudes and behavior we have considered to this point.

Notes

1. Cohen, Nisbett, Bowdle, and Schwarz, in press.

2. The correlation for the two observers' judgments for amusement was .52, $p < .001$ and for anger was .57, $p < .001$.

3. The debriefer explained why the research was important and why the deception and insult were used. Informal conversations made it clear that subjects were not unhappy with the treatment accorded them. When asked to rate how interesting the experiment was and how glad they were to have been in it, the modal answer was seven on

a seven-point scale for both questions. On every measure, insulted subjects were actually more favorable toward the experiment than controls.

4. Mean amusement ratings for northerners = 2.77, for southerners = 1.74, $t(41)$ = 2.85, $p < .01$.

5. Mean anger rating for northerners = 2.34, for southerners = 3.05, $t(41)$ = 1.61, .10 $< p < .15$.

6. There were no significant differences in how aroused, flustered, resigned, or wary subjects seemed (all $ts < 1.1$, all $ps > .25$).

7. Chi-square $(1, N = 40) = 12.13, p < .001$.

8. To examine the statistical interaction between region and insult, we performed an analysis of variance on a three-level variable (no violence, violence suggested, actual violence). Higher numbers indicated greater violence. The means were: southern insult = 2.30, southern control = 1.40, northern insult = 1.73, northern control = 2.05 (interaction $F(1,78) = 7.65, p < .005$).

9. Booth et al., 1989; Dabbs and Hooper, 1990; Kirschbaum, Bartussek, and Strasburger, 1992; Leshner, 1983; Popp and Baum, 1989; Thompson, 1988.

10. Booth et al., 1989; Dabbs, 1992; Elias, 1981; Gladue, 1991; Gladue, Boechler, and McCaul, 1989; Kemper, 1990; Mazur, 1985; Mazur and Lamb, 1980; Olweus, 1986; Popp and Baum, 1989.

11. Booth et al., 1989; Campbell, O'Rourke, and Rabow, 1988, cited in Mazur, Booth, and Dabbs, 1992; Dabbs, 1992; Mazur, 1985; Mazur, Booth, and Dabbs, 1992; see also Gladue, Boechler, and McCaul, 1989, p. 416; but see Salvador et al., 1987.

12. Osborne, Niekrasz, and Seale, 1993.

13. The subject was told to continue to chew the sugarless gum as he walked down the hall to deposit his questionnaire and was told not to talk while he had the gum in his mouth. This was to keep the subject from talking to observers after the insult in the public condition. The public observers rated the subject's emotional reaction to the bump. (No private observation could be made since there were no observers in the hall for the private bump in Experiment 2.) Emotion ratings in the public condition of Experiment 2 (and in the public and private conditions of Experiment 3, reported further on) yielded weak and inconsistent results regarding reaction to the bump. We believe this was because of the requirements to chew gum and not to talk in Experiments 2 and 3, which prohibited the free expression of emotion. But of course, this is a post-hoc explanation, and the results of Experiment 1 regarding anger and amusement must be treated with caution until subsequent research replicates the findings of Experiment 1 in ecologically natural circumstances. More complete details on the results of the emotion ratings can be found in Cohen, 1994.

14. Samples were frozen at $-30°C$ ($-20°F$), so that they could be assayed by [125] I radioimmuno-assay (Diagnostic Products Corporation) by technicians of the University of Michigan Reproductive Science Program.

15. $t(165) = 2.14, p < .03$. For the sake of consistency, the interaction contrast specified was +3 (for the insulted southerner condition) vs. $-1, -1, -1$ (for all other conditions) for all analyses in Experiments 2 and 3 (though it did not always capture the actual pattern of the data optimally). An overall "politeness index," adding scores on all behavioral measures in Study 3, showed control southern subjects to be somewhat more deferential than control northern subjects ($p < .08$).

16. $t(165) = 2.19, p < .03$.

17. There was one other measure in Experiment 2. In a situation designed to elicit demonstrations of toughness, subjects were asked to volunteer to take electric shock. They chose the level of shock they wanted to take, once in front of two other subjects (actually confederates), and later when given a private opportunity to reconsider their choice after the two other subjects had left the room. Overall, southern subjects elected to take more shock in front of the two other people than they did in private, whereas that was not true for northerners. However, this effect held for *all* southerners, not just insulted southerners. (Complete details on the shock procedure can be found in Cohen et al., 1995.) In Experiment 3, we allowed subjects a more natural way to demonstrate toughness and dominance, hoping that would differentiate the insulted southerners from the noninsulted southerners and from both groups of northerners.

18. $t(142) = 3.45$, $p < 001$.

19. $t(144) = 1.89$, $p < .06$.

20. $t(144) = 2.52$, $p < .01$.

21. $t(144) = 2.53$, $p < .01$. Southern subjects regarded the damage to their reputations as being limited to character traits having to do with masculinity, such as "strong-weak" and "cowardly-courageous." The public insult did not differentially affect how northerners and southerners thought the other person saw them on *nonmasculine* dimensions. Moreover, the insult had little effect on how the subject rated *himself* on all dimensions. For all groups that were insulted—including publicly insulted southerners—subjects' self-ratings (on both the macho and nonmacho items) were about the same and were not different from those of subjects who were not insulted.

5

Collective Expressions
of the Culture of Honor:
Violence, Social Policy, and the Law

Wᴇ ʜᴀᴠᴇ ᴀʀɢᴜᴇᴅ that the high homicide rates of the South reflect values
of self-protection, sensitivity to insult, and willingness to take matters of punishment into one's own hands. The evidence for this is that these values are expressed in surveys of southerners' attitudes and revealed by physiological and
behavioral responses examined in laboratory situations. Are these values also
manifested in aggregate, institutional-level processes that have been called
"collective representations"[1] or "public representations"?[2] In particular, are
these values encoded in laws and reflected in the administration of social policies? In this chapter we ask these questions for several domains—legal codes,
case law, systems of justice, political legislation, media representations, and institutional behavior. We used both field experiments and archival research
methods to answer these questions.

Cultural Differences in Collective Expressions

Studying collective expressions is necessary to back up our claim, which is not
just that there are more violent individuals and violent acts in the South, but
also that southern *culture* is more violent than northern *culture* in matters
where honor is concerned. This level of analysis requires us to go beyond the
individual and look toward the collectivity in our research questions and methods, in an effort to show that there are more institutional and social supports
for violence. Thus, it is important to show that the differences we have outlined
hold at the level of law, policy, and public action.

In addition, it is important to examine these issues not just because of what laws, policies, and other public representations *are* but because of what they *do*. "Statecraft is soulcraft";[3] and the purpose of law and social policy is to shape the behavior of citizens by defining what is acceptable, appropriate, worthy of reward, and worthy of punishment. Thus, these collective expressions feed back and affect individual behavior and attitudes (though not always in the way intended). The following hypotheses, for example, seem plausible: Loose gun control laws reinforce as well as reflect the frontier mentality; laws allowing capital punishment legitimize retributive feelings; corporal punishment laws convey ideas about appropriate methods for socializing children and dealing with disorder; media portrayals of violence as being justified encourage acceptance of violence. Even individual behavior, if it occurs in an institutional context and is seen as "official," can serve to create or reinforce public representations of what is right, good, and appropriate.

Given the evidence so far, what would we expect about differences between regions concerning public representations? We might anticipate that laws, social policies, and other aggregate behaviors would differ among regions, with the South showing a greater preference for violence for purposes of self-protection and maintaining honor. We would also expect the West to share, at least to some degree, the ideology of the South and thus to have similar public representations.

Much of the West was initially settled by herding people of southern origin, and the frontier undoubtedly played as large a role in forming the western mentality as the southern. As we have noted in earlier chapters, there is empirical evidence that the West resembles the South in its stance toward violence. Homicide rates of the West, presented in Chapter 2, are partway between those of the South on the one hand and the Northeast and Midwest on the other. Some attitudes toward violence also show the West to be intermediate between the South and other regions on many issues. Westerners resemble southerners in their belief about the importance of weapons for self-protection, for example. Items from several surveys that separate the West from the rest of the Non-South showed that westerners—especially mountain-state westerners—resembled southerners in many respects.

In one of the few studies exploring regional differences in violent practices, Baron and Straus created an index of "legitimate violence."[4] This index was composed of measures such as national guard expenditures, corporal punishment laws, execution rates, and per capita production of college football players. They found that by those indicators the West was at least as fond of violence as the South.

One possible exception to the generalization that the West resembles the South concerns issues of violence for purposes of control. The South, unlike the West, was shaped by the institution of slavery, which was maintained through violence and the threat of violence, both individual and collective. "The fact of force . . . pervaded the slave relationship. It was there, implicit or explicit, from the instant of purchase to the instant of death."[5]

The lesson of slavery (and post–Civil War race relations), that violence can be used to control, could be extended. That is, if violence could be used by a man to control his slaves, it could also be used to control others that "belonged" to him—like women and children. Old southern statutes and case law even specify that violence may be an appropriate "correction" for a slave, a child, or a wife.[6] For example, in the Tennessee case of *Jacob v. State,* the right of a master to physically "correct" a slave is likened to rights in relationships of "a kindred character, [between] master and apprentice, schoolmaster and scholar, parent and child, officer and prisoner."[7] The North Carolina Supreme Court came to a similar conclusion in 1874 regarding rights in a husband-wife relationship: "If no permanent injury has been inflicted, nor malice, cruelty nor dangerous violence shown by the husband, it is better to draw the curtain, shut out the public gaze, and leave the parties to forget and forgive."[8] With this history of slavery and coercive control, one would expect the South to have laws more tolerant of domestic violence, capital punishment, and corporal punishment than the West, which had no history of slavery.

In sum, we might expect both southern and western states to be approving of violence used for protective purposes and in defense of honor, but the legacy of slavery should make the South also more inclined to favor violence in the service of social order or hierarchy maintenance. To pursue these hypotheses, we studied four social policy issues on which we expected that the South and West would resemble each other and differ from the North. The issues related to defense of self and property: gun control; the so-called retreat rule in cases of self-defense, requiring that an individual flee from a potential assailant to avoid killing him; the legitimacy of the use of force in defense of home and property; and support for national defense efforts. Statistical tests for these issues involved contrasts between the South and West on the one hand and the North on the other. Three issues relating to coercive control were also studied: the proprietary right to control of the family by violence as indicated by domestic violence statutes, the acceptance of corporal punishment in the schools, and the use of the death penalty. The North and West° could be expected to resemble each other on these issues and differ from the South. Statistical tests for these issues involved contrasts between the South on the one hand and the West and North on the other. All contrasts reported are statistically significant unless otherwise stated.[9]

°In the studies that follow, definitions of the various regions follow U.S. Census classification. The South was defined as census divisions 5, 6, and 7, excluding Washington, D.C., as in Chapters 2, 3, and 4. The West was defined as census divisions 8 and 9, excluding Alaska and Hawaii. This includes New Mexico, Arizona, Colorado, Utah, Nevada, Wyoming, Idaho, Montana, California, Oregon, and Washington. All other states, encompassing New England, the Mid-Atlantic and the Midwest, are called the "North" for reasons of brevity.

Laws Pertaining to Violence for Protective Purposes and Defense of Honor

Gun Control

Where the frontier mentality remains strong, the gun should be seen less as a dangerous weapon to be kept out of people's hands than as a necessary instrument of self-protection for law-abiding citizens—the "great equalizer" in the war against criminals.[10] In regions where the frontier mentality is not so firmly entrenched, the idea of the weapon as a "peacemaker" may simply seem absurd. It will be recalled from Chapter 3 that the South and the West remain the regions where people are most likely to report owning or carrying a gun or other weapon for protection.

To examine how cultural differences with respect to guns are embodied in laws, we analyzed state gun control laws summarized by the National Rifle Association (NRA).[11] We also examined how U.S. senators and representatives voted on key issues identified by the pro–gun control group Handgun Control Incorporated (HCI). Finally, we examined campaign contributions given to federal legislators from the political action committees of the NRA and HCI. Both the South and West, because of their frontier heritage, could be expected to be more anti–gun control than the North.

State Gun Control Laws.   The NRA evaluated state laws regulating the purchase and ownership of handguns on several dimensions, for example, whether handguns had to be registered.[12] On each of the items, the South and West were looser in their regulation of guns than the North. The northern states on average had more than one-third of the possible regulations, whereas southern and western ones had only about one-tenth, as may be seen in Figure 5.1.

Legislators' Voting on Federal Gun Laws.   Handgun Control Incorporated compiled a list of how legislators voted on what HCI identified as key gun issues, for example, regulating the interstate sale and transport of handguns.[13] As may be seen in Figure 5.2, legislators from the North were more in favor of gun control than legislators from the South and West. This was true both in the Senate, where the South and West were quite different from the North, and in the House.[14]

As would be expected, patterns reflecting those voting records are found when one examines monetary contributions to legislators from the political action funds of the National Rifle Association and Handgun Control Incorporated for legislators in office from 1985 to 1992, the period when these votes took place.

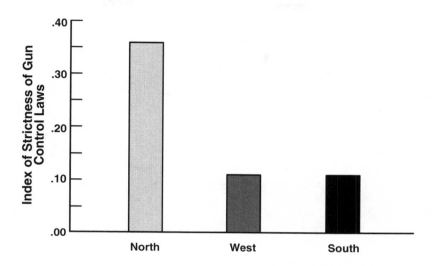

FIGURE 5.1   Strictness of gun control laws in the North, West, and South in 1992. Source: National Rifle Association, 1992.

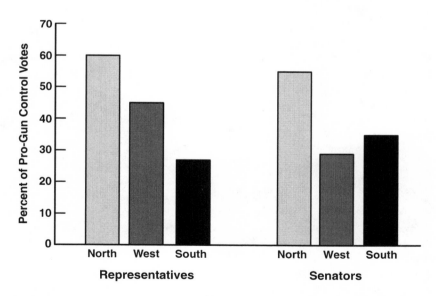

FIGURE 5.2   Percent of pro–gun control votes in the House of Representatives and the Senate from 1985 to 1991, by region. Source: Handgun Control Incorporated.

Laws Pertaining to Self-Defense

Frontier mythology, like that of other cultures of honor, glorified the person who stood up for his rights and would not back down or hide if attacked. Though one might have escaped safely and avoided the necessity of killing, it would have been cowardly and dishonorable to flee. Instead, according to frontier lore, a real man was obliged to stand his ground and, if necessary, kill his assailant.[15]

Retreat Rules.   The question of obligation to retreat lies at the base of a major split in the history of American self-defense law.[16] The split is between states that have adopted the "retreat rule," requiring an innocent person to retreat if possible before killing an assailant, and states that have adopted the "true man rule," allowing a person to stand fast in the face of an attack and kill the assailant if necessary.[17]

A major argument against the requirement of retreat is that it would be "cowardly and dishonorable, not befitting a true man of courage"[18] and as such it would be wrong for the law to make "one act in a cowardly or humiliating role."[19] This argument makes explicit appeal to the notion of "honor" as a reputation for strength and toughness.[20]

In addition to requiring retreat, some states do not allow an actor to use deadly force if the actor can avoid it "by surrendering possession of a thing to a person asserting a claim of right thereto [surrender of property] or by complying with a demand that he abstain from any action which he has no duty to take [compliance with demand]."[21]

Our examination of state laws revealed clear differences on all dimensions regarding retreat issues. As may be seen in Figure 5.3, the northern states were more likely to have either specific statutes or case law requiring retreat, more likely to have a "surrender of property" requirement, and more likely to have a "compliance with demand" requirement than either southern or western states.

Defense of Home and Property.   We also examined a few provisions in state statutes pertaining to defense of home and property. In particular, we examined whether state statutes: (1) specifically entitle citizens to "absolute safety" in their own homes; (2) declare that a person using deadly force in defense of his or her own home would be "presumed" by law to be acting reasonably; and (3) mandate that before using force in defense of property, one must first request the offending person "to desist from his interference with the property" (unless such a request would be useless or dangerous). This three-item index (with the third item reverse-scored) showed that southern and western states were more accepting of people's use of force to defend their home and property than northern states were.[22]

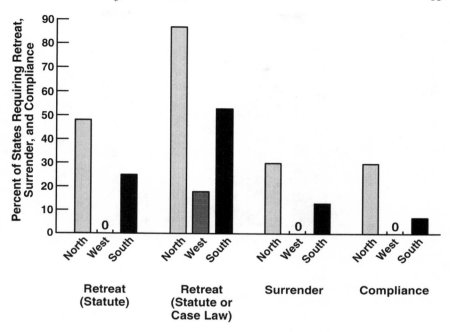

FIGURE 5.3 Percent of states in each region requiring retreat, surrender, and compliance to demands rather than killing an assailant. Source: Cohen, 1995.

In sum, we found that, for all measures, the South and West give citizens more freedom to use violence in defending themselves, their homes, and their property. The self-defense laws plausibly reflect the frontier development of these regions and the culture-of-honor tradition of protection in the absence of strong law enforcement.

National Defense Policy

When people consider violence between nations, they often make analogies to violence between individuals. For example, war is often justified in terms of protection of the nation and in terms of national honor. It is not surprising then to learn that southern leaders often rallied support for the Civil War by appeals to defense of southern honor and manhood.[23]

Assuming that people extend their reasoning about individual self-defense to national self-defense, we anticipated that southerners and westerners would be more in favor of various strong national defense initiatives than northerners. To test this, we examined key votes of legislators listed in the *Almanac of American Politics 1992*[24] and divided the votes into those on issues related to national defense and those not related to national defense.

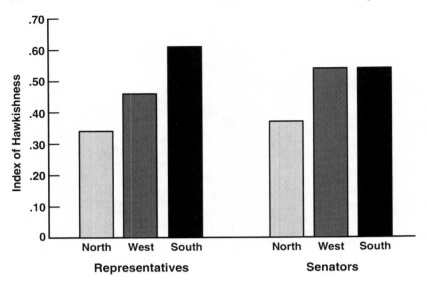

FIGURE 5.4   Index of pro–national defense votes in the House of Representatives and the Senate in 1989–1990, by region. Source: Barone and Ujifusa, 1991.

Key National Defense Votes. In the House of Representatives, there were four key national defense votes during 1989–1990 identified by the *Almanac* (for example, votes to "decrease funds for the Strategic Defense Initiative to $3.1 billion" and to "urge the President to negotiate a prohibition on nuclear weapons testing").[25] To this list was added whether the Representative voted to authorize U.S. force in the Gulf War.[26] (For each vote, legislators were given a one if they voted "hawkishly" and a zero if they did not, and an index was computed.) As may be seen in Figure 5.4, representatives from the South were most hawkish, followed by those of the West, with those of the North last. (The West was significantly different from both the North and the South.)

In the Senate, there were also four key national defense votes. (These included votes to "table a proposal to cut the Strategic Defense Initiative to $3.95 billion" and to "cancel procurement funds for two B-2 Stealth bombers."[27]) How the senator voted on the Gulf War was also added to the index. On all 5 votes, senators from the South and West were the most hawkish, as may be seen in Figure 5.4.

Foreign Policy Ratings.   Consistent with the key voting records, legislators of the South, and to a lesser extent those of the West, were given higher ratings on the National Security Index of the American Security Council, as may be seen in Figure 5.5.[28] (In the House, the West was significantly or marginally

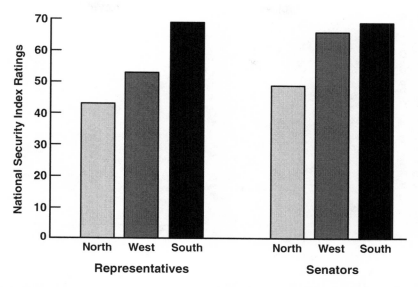

FIGURE 5.5   Scores on National Security Index of the American Security Council for legislators in the House of Representatives and the Senate in 1990, by region. Source: Barone and Ujifusa, 1991.

significantly different from both the North and the South.) Thus regional patterns are evident in legislative behavior, consistent with the notion that the South and West would have a more pro-military stance than the North.

Laws Pertaining to Issues of Social Control

We next turn to issues of violence, for which southerners can be expected to differ not only from northerners but from westerners as well. Because of the South's history of slavery, southerners might find the notion of violence for purposes of social control and hierarchy maintenance more attractive than do either northerners or westerners.

Domestic Violence

Men use violence not only to protect their castle from those outside it but also to control those within it. Such violence has often had legal, religious, and philosophical approval.[29] British common law of the eighteenth century, for example, adopted the "rule of thumb" allowing a husband to "beat his wife with a 'rod not thicker than his thumb.'"[30] In the United States, a Mississippi court set the precedent for allowing corporal punishment of wives by husbands in 1824.[31] And it was not until 1882 that Maryland became the first state to pass a law criminalizing wife beating. Ironically, it was punishable by "40 lashes or a

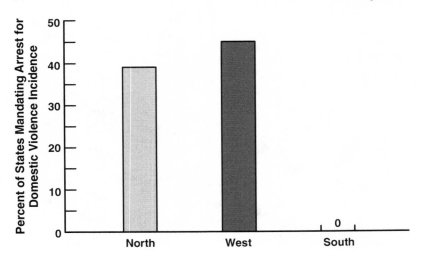

FIGURE 5.6   Percent of states in each region mandating arrest for a domestic violence incident. Source: National Center on Women and Family Law, 1991, updated 1993.

year in jail."[32] Historically, violence by men against their wives was often "deemed necessary for the 'well-being' of women."[33]

Men use violence against their wives as a way of coercing them, establishing control, and "conveying rules to regulate 'proper' female behavior."[34] In the view of Daly and Wilson[35] and other scholars, violence against women often revolves around control of the woman's sexuality—as men use violence in response to real or imaginary infidelities.

To examine how state laws treat domestic violence we focused on the issues of mandatory arrest and child custody codes. Since control is a central issue in domestic violence, the South could be expected to be more lenient with domestic violence offenders. Statistical comparisons thus contrasted the South with the North and West.

Having obtained a list of states that have mandatory arrest laws from the National Center on Women and Family Law in New York, we found a dramatic regional difference in the percent of states mandating arrest for a domestic violence incident. As may be seen in Figure 5.6, about 40 percent of northern and western states mandated arrest for a domestic violence incident but not a single southern state did so.

Custody codes and their relationship to domestic violence were also examined along several dimensions described by Hart (for example, whether custody codes "require courts to consider domestic violence when fashioning custody and visitation awards").[36] For the five dimensions offered by Hart, states

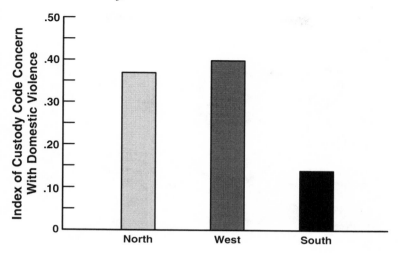

FIGURE 5.7   Index of custody code concern with domestic violence, by region.
Source: Hart, 1992.

were given a score of one if they addressed domestic violence on a given dimension and zero if they did not. Along all dimensions, custody codes in the South appeared less likely to address domestic violence by limiting the rights of abusing parents. Averaged across items, the difference on the custody code index, as seen in Figure 5.7, was highly significant.

Corporal Punishment

According to opinion surveys, as we saw in Chapter 3, southerners are much more likely than nonsoutherners to advocate spanking to discipline their children. We might expect that spanking would also be seen as an appropriate disciplinary tool when carried out by a "legitimate" authority like a school official. Indeed, corporal punishment is known to be more likely to be administered in southern schools.[37]

We add to that body of evidence an examination of recent state corporal punishment laws and a 1990 survey of corporal punishment rates. We obtained from the National Coalition to Abolish Corporal Punishment in Schools a list of states that banned corporal punishment. As may be seen in Figure 5.8, the list of states prohibiting corporal punishment included very few southern states and a much higher percentage of western and northern states.

Data were also obtained from the Department of Education's Office of Civil Rights, and the percent of students given corporal punishment in their sample of schools during the 1989–1990 school year was computed. As may be seen in

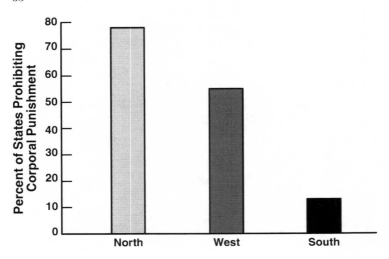

FIGURE 5.8   Percent of states in each region prohibiting corporal punishment in the schools. Source: National Coalition to Abolish Corporal Punishment in Schools, 1993.

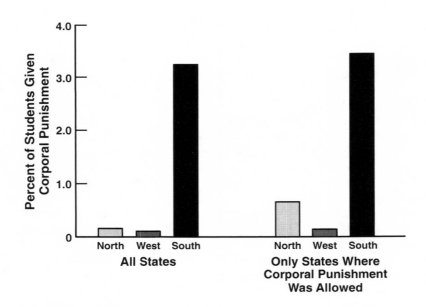

FIGURE 5.9   Percent of students in region given corporal punishment during the 1989–1990 school year. Source: U.S. Department of Education, 1992.

Figure 5.9, the South far outpaced other regions in administering corporal punishment. This conclusion remained true when analyses were examined separately for whites, minorities, males, or females and when analyses were conducted separately just for those states allowing corporal punishment.

Capital Punishment

Capital punishment can be regarded as an extreme form of violence for purposes of control. Thus it might be expected that different regions would have different attitudes toward capital punishment. In fact, however, in each region of the country, about 70 percent of the population say that they support the death penalty.[38]

This failure to find regional differences in attitude may not be quite so damaging for our hypothesis as might be assumed. Phoebe Ellsworth and Lee Ross have shown that there can be a gross inconsistency between attitudes toward the death penalty in general and preference for its use in particular cases.[39] The same people who describe themselves as being in favor of capital punishment in the abstract are often unwilling to vote for a death sentence when asked about specific cases, even when the cases involve heinous capital crimes. Such findings indicate that people's attitudes toward capital punishment may be essentially *symbolic:* The existence of laws allowing capital punishment is satisfying, but their use may be disturbing. Analogously, at the institutional or collective level, regional differences may exist in the actual use of capital punishment even if there are weaker differences in the extent to which laws permit executions.

We looked at three stages in the process of carrying out an execution. First, of course, a state must have a capital punishment law. Second, prosecutors, jurors, and judges must be willing to seek, recommend, and hand down the death penalty in particular cases. Third, once a death sentence is given, the case must work its way through the appellate process, where the sentence may be overturned; thus, many convicted persons will be sentenced to death row but never executed. Our initial expectation was that for all these measures of state-mandated violence for purposes of control, the South would differ from other regions of the country. As will be seen, the results depart in interesting ways from this expectation.

We examined data provided by the Bureau of Justice Statistics in the *Capital Punishment 1991* bulletin, which revealed that southern and western states are far more likely to have capital punishment statutes. As may be seen in the top left panel of Figure 5.10, all but one southern state (West Virginia) have capital punishment laws; but the West is fully as favorable toward capital punishment, as indicated by possession of such laws. By contrast, only ten of twenty-three northern states (43 percent) allow capital punishment. Similarly, like southern states, western states are more likely to sentence murderers to the death penalty when it is an available option, as may be seen in the top right panel of Figure 5.10.

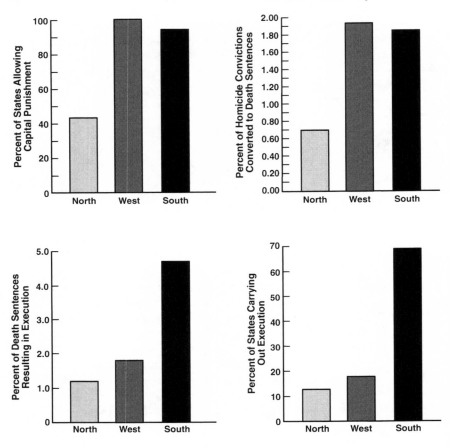

FIGURE 5.10   (Clockwise from upper left) Percent of states allowing capital punishment, percent of homicide convictions converted to death sentences, percent of death sentences resulting in execution, and percent of states carrying out an execution. Source: U.S. Department of Justice (1992).

But when we turn to the third and most crucial question—that of executions actually carried out—the South differs clearly from the other two regions. A higher percentage of convicted murderers are executed in the South, and a much higher fraction of southern states had executed at least one individual than northern or western states had, as may be seen in the bottom two panels of Figure 5.10.

The difference in the ratio of persons executed to persons sentenced to death is interesting because it suggests something about southern and non-southern legal systems and institutions. Whether the condemned prisoner actually lives or dies is not decided by a jury but by attorneys, courts, interest groups, and politicians, who may prevent or facilitate the execution. The greater ratio of executions to death sentences in the South suggests that southern legal systems (broadly defined) are more willing to carry out the death penalty than other legal systems after a capital sentence is imposed. This probably explains why, of the 157 executions from 1977 to 1991, 140 were in the South. Taken as a whole, the data leave us with some interesting speculations about the nature of cultural differences concerning capital punishment that exist among regions. Both the South and the West are likely to make capital punishment possible by statute and by court action, but only the South is likely to actually carry it out. Our guess is that a collective version of the *symbolic* function of capital punishment exists. The West, like the South, has capital punishment laws and hands down the death penalty. But only the South seems to have the means and desire for actually executing its prisoners.

Public Representations of Honor, Control, and Violence

The frontier legacy of the South and West legitimized self-protective or defensive violence, but the slave system of the South also legitimized violence for the purpose of discipline, control, and punishment. We have shown that contemporary regional differences at the collective level reflect these stances toward violence.

Consistent with an emphasis on the citizens' role in protecting themselves, the South and West are more libertarian in their gun control regulations and have legal codes reflecting a greater approval of violence for self-defense. Analogously, elites of the South and West show more support for strong national defense policies.

Consistent with the notion that southerners are more accepting of violence for purposes of control, the South has laws more lenient toward domestic violence, is more tolerant of corporal punishment in the schools, and has systems of justice more willing to carry out executions.

Slavery and Disciplinary Violence. In addition to the South-versus-West comparisons, there is more evidence that the legacy of slavery legitimized disciplinary violence. That is, if we look within the South, those states that had a higher proportion of slaves in 1860 are today more in favor of disciplinary violence than states that had a lower proportion of slaves. Thus, states of the slave South were between two and four times more likely to administer corporal punishment than states of the nonslave South, according to the 1990 data. And when it comes to capital punishment, states of the slave South were three times more likely to have executed someone than states of the nonslave South, during the period 1977 to 1991. Results were particularly striking when we looked at the chance that a prisoner on death row would eventually be executed. The chance of a death row prisoner being executed were up to *fifty* times greater in the slave

South than the nonslave South. As we would predict, the differences between the slave and nonslave South were restricted to coercive, disciplinary violence; the two regions of the South did not differ when it came to defensive violence.

That the West and nonslave South were more likely to have capital punishment laws and to hand out death sentences than the North—but not more likely to actually execute people—gives us interesting parallels at the collective level to important individual-level phenomena. These phenomena are (1) the distinction between symbolic and instrumental attitudes drawn by theorists such as Daniel Katz, David Sears, and Donald Kinder[40] and (2) the classic distinction in social psychology between expressed attitudes and actual behavior.

Symbolic Versus Actual Violence.   Sears and Kinder described symbolic attitudes as "almost wholly abstract, ideological, and symbolic in nature."[41] Such attitudes are not concrete, instrumental, or goal oriented but are expressive of values. They "have almost no conceivable personal relevance to the individual, but have to do with his moral code or his sense of how society should be organized."[42]

Symbolic public representations may serve a very similar function on a cultural level. They are above all expressive of a culture's values, but they may not have many practical implications or much tangible relevance. On the collective level, that may be particularly true of issues like capital punishment. Collectively as well as individually, most Americans like *the idea of having a death penalty* but do not actually like to see it used.[43]

Attitudes Versus Behavior.   The distinction on the public level between symbolic and actual violence also parallels the attitude-behavior distinction on the private level. Social psychologists have repeatedly demonstrated that attitudes are often poor predictors of behavior. If an individual does not have a behavioral intention, a plan for acting on an attitude, or a "channel" through which a prescribed behavior can be enacted, an attitude may not translate well into behavior. Similarly, on a collective level, if a culture does not have systems and institutional supports for making things happen, procedures for accomplishing social goals, or "gatekeepers" willing to execute policies, the symbolic attitudes that are enshrined in law and official policy may not translate into effective action.

Perhaps that is one reason why the West and nonslave South are high on the symbolic approval of violence for social control but not on the practical implementation of it, whereas the slave South is high on both. It is possible that the practical demands on southerners of forcibly maintaining a slave and caste system created the institutions, procedures, and actors capable of carrying out real violence. In the absence of such requirements, the West and nonslave South did not develop the same sorts of channels for using violence for social control.

Thus, there are distinct parallels between individual- and aggregate-level phenomena. Just as individual attitudes and behaviors can have symbolic and instrumental meanings, so too can collective behaviors. And just as there can be strong discrepancies between attitudes and behaviors at the individual level, that can also be true at the collective level. At the intersection of these individual and collective levels is the behavior of individuals acting in an institutional context—the subject we turn to next.

Though behavior is performed by individuals, it can take on quite important cultural meanings when people act in their institutional roles. Not only are the personal outcomes of involved individuals directly affected, but there can be implications for the collective as well. Institutional policies (formal or informal) and public representations and norms are established or strengthened. Actions thus can take on the imprimatur of cultural approval when people act in their "official" capacities.

We conducted two field experiments in which we explored how individuals acting in their institutional roles can reflect their cultures in ways that have consequences for public representations. We examined how honor-related crimes of violence would be treated by potential employers in the South and West versus the North and how they would be portrayed by the media of these regions.

Field Experiments Examining Institutional Behavior

In Experiment 1, we tested the possibility that employers in the South and West might respond more favorably than those of the North to a job applicant who had committed an act of honor-related violence. In Experiment 2, we examined the possibility that the media in the South and West would be more sympathetic to honor-related violence and thus that newspapers in those regions would write stories about honor-related violence that were more sympathetic to the perpetrator than newspapers in the North.[44]

Field Experiment 1: Honor, Violence, and Forgiveness

In Experiment 1, we sent out letters to employers across the country, inquiring about a job. All letters were from an "applicant" who described himself as a hard-working, 27-year-old man who was relocating to the area from Michigan and who listed appropriate qualifications. There was one blemish, however, on these otherwise very solid letters. For half the letters, the third paragraph read:

> There is one thing I must explain, because I feel I must be honest and want no misunderstandings. I have been convicted of a felony, namely manslaughter. You will probably want an explanation for this before you send me an application, so I will provide it. I got into a fight with someone who was having an affair with my fiancée. I lived in a small town, and one night this person confronted me in front of my friends at the bar. He told everyone that he and my fiancée were sleeping together. He laughed at me to my face and asked me to step outside if I was man enough. I

was young and didn't want to back down from a challenge in front of everyone. As we went into the alley, he started to attack me. He knocked me down, and he picked up a bottle. I could have run away and the judge said I should have, but my pride wouldn't let me. Instead I picked up a pipe that was laying in the alley and hit him with it. I didn't mean to kill him, but he died a few hours later at the hospital.

For the other half of the letters (the control letters), the third paragraph read:

There is one thing I must explain, because I feel I must be honest and I want no misunderstandings. I have been convicted of a felony, namely motor vehicle theft. You will probably want an explanation for this before you send me an application, so I will provide it. I have no excuse for my behavior. I was young and I needed money. I had a wife and kids and by stealing a couple of expensive cars, I was able to give them what I always needed to give them and pay off the bills I owed. I never intended to cause the car owners any serious trouble. I was sentenced for grand theft auto and am very sorry for my crime. I was desperate but now I realize this is no excuse.

In all the letters, the fourth paragraph read: "I realize that what I did was wrong. ..."

The 912 letters were sent to businesses that were part of five chains, with stores located around the country. These national chains included: a general merchandise store chain, a low-end motel chain, a high-end hotel chain, a family restaurant chain, and a motorcycle dealership chain.[45] The prediction was that employers of the South and West would be more likely than those of the North to be sympathetic and cooperative in response to the homicide letter, whereas there would be little or no regional difference for the control letter.

We analyzed the 112 responses (1) for how cooperative they were in complying with the "applicant's" requests (whether they included an application, name of a contact person, a phone number for the contact person, hours or days to stop by, a business card, and a note or letter with their response); and (2) for the tone of the note or letter if one was included (how encouraging the letter was, how understanding it was, how personal it was, and whether it mentioned an appreciation for the applicant's candor).

As may be seen in Figure 5.11, in response to the homicide letter, southern and western employers were indeed more likely to be compliant with the applicant's requests than northern employers were, and no regional differences were found for the control letter. And as may be seen in Figure 5.12, in response to the homicide applicant, the tone of the letter from southern and western employers was more likely to be sympathetic, compared to northern employers. Again, no differences were found on the control letter.

A qualitative example might help to make the data more vivid. In response to the man who had killed his provoker, one southern employer wrote back that although she had no jobs, she was quite sympathetic:

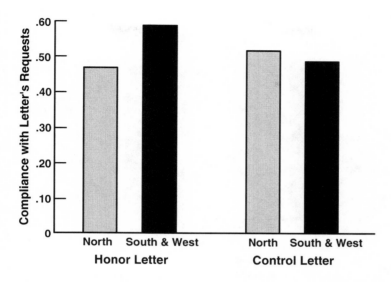

FIGURE 5.11 Compliance with job applicant's requests in the North and in the South and West when he reported an honor-related versus a non-honor-related felony. Source: Cohen and Nisbett, 1995.

As for your problem of the past, anyone could probably be in the situation you were in. It was just an unfortunate incident that shouldn't be held against you. Your honesty shows that you are sincere. . . .

I wish you the best of luck for your future. You have a positive attitude and a willingness to work. Those are the qualities that businesses look for in an employee. Once you get settled, if you are near here, please stop in and see us.

No letter from a northern employer was so sympathetic toward the man who had killed in defense of his honor.

Field Experiment 2:
Provocation and Just Cause for Violence

In Experiment 2, we tried to show that the media of the South and West would treat honor-related violence more sympathetically than would the media of the North—even given the same "objective" facts. To keep control over the set of facts, we sent out a "fact sheet" description of a fictitious honor-related stabbing to newspapers in the North, West, and South. Personnel at the newspapers—who were aware that the case was hypothetical—were asked to turn the events into a story (for pay) as it would appear in their paper. (College newspa-

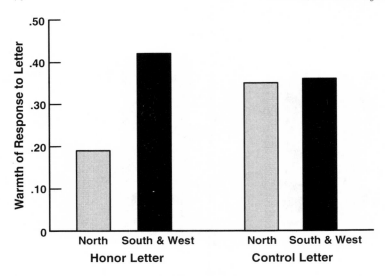

Figure 5.12   Warmth of response to job applicant's letter in the North and in the South and West when he reported an honor-related versus a non-honor-related felony. Source: Cohen and Nisbett, 1995.

pers rather than "professional" newspapers were used in this study in an attempt to get a higher compliance rate.) The prediction was that newspapers in the South and West would describe the offender more sympathetically and would describe the stabbing as more provoked and less aggravated than papers in the North would. A control story—involving a crime of violence not related to honor—provided for a tighter test of the hypothesis.

The following is a brief summary of facts relevant for culture-of-honor concerns:

Victor Jensen (a 28-year-old Caucasian) stabbed Martin Shell (a 27-year-old Caucasian) at a party.

According to witnesses: Shell spilled a glass of beer on Jensen's pants.

The two began arguing and had to be separated.

Shell shouted that Jensen's sister, Ann, was "a slut."

Several men were heard to make comments about what they would do if someone said that about their sister.

Jensen left the party. As he left, Shell and his friends laughed at Jensen. Shell then shouted that both Jensen's sister and mother were "sluts."

Jensen returned to the party ten minutes later. He demanded that Shell take back his comments "or else." Shell laughed at Jensen and said, "Or else what, Rambo?"

Jensen then pulled a four-inch knife out of his jacket and stabbed Shell twice. Shell was unarmed at the time of the stabbing.

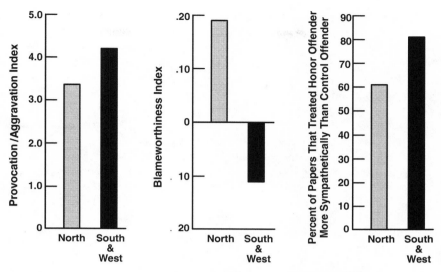

Figure 5.13   Provocation/aggravation index, blameworthiness index, and percent of newspaper stories that treated honor offender more sympathetically than control offender, by region of paper. Source: Cohen and Nisbett, 1995.

Again, many other facts were included on the fact sheet but the above incidents highlight the culture-of-honor issues. The control story described violence committed by a character named Hansen (also a Caucasian) as he pistol-whipped a clerk at a convenience store.

The stories written by staff at the 94 responding papers were analyzed on several dimensions.[46] A provocation/aggravation index was computed. It considered things Shell had done to provoke Jensen (spilling beer on Jensen, insulting his sister, laughing at him, and so on) relative to aggravating circumstances of Jensen's crime (for example, that Jensen returned ten minutes later with a knife, suggesting premeditation, that he stabbed Shell *twice*, and that Shell was unarmed). Compared to northern papers, southern and western papers, as may be seen in Figure 5.13, were more likely to emphasize provoking circumstances than aggravating ones. On several other indicators of blame and fault, southern and western papers were also less likely than northern papers to see Jensen as blameworthy for stabbing Shell. And consistent with these results, newspapers in the South and West were more likely to portray the offender in the honor-related story (Jensen) as more sympathetic than the offender in the non-honor-related story (Hansen).

Few of the miscellaneous facts not related to culture-of-honor issues and few of the facts in the control story differed by region. Furthermore, demographically, with respect to the circulation of the papers, the age of the reporters, or the sex of the reporters writing the story, there was little difference between regions.[47]

The striking differences in the reporting of the honor-related story illustrate one way that institutions can help perpetuate the culture of honor. Much has been written about how the media promote violence by showing it as a legitimate or even heroic solution to problems. Field Experiment 2 shows that there are clear cultural differences in how papers of the South and West versus the North present such violence to readers. The private representations of the reporter thus become public representations in line with cultural norms, which may then push readers' private representations still further in that direction.

Newspapers are just one source of collective storytelling, however. It seems remarkable that such clear, consistent differences were found, given that the same facts were presented to all newspapers—institutions that are supposed to report stories objectively and according to formula. One can only imagine what would happen on the next iterations—as readers who are not bound by the journalist's sense of objectivity and closeness to the facts retell the story to others, who then retell the story to still others. As this game of "telephone" continues and stories spread through a community, it seems likely that the stories would stray further and further from the given facts, becoming molded into myths of an ever more culturally prescribed sort. These communal myths would both reflect the biases of the culture and perpetuate the culture.

Social scientists have only begun to explore the way cultures persist and evolve. At this point, all we can do is speculate, but it seems quite plausible that there is a feedback loop between individual- and collective-level behaviors that helps keep a culture strong. Private representations can create public representations that feed back and further influence private representations.[48] The laws and institutional behaviors we studied seem like good examples of how a culture-of-honor ideology can be manifested at a collective level and then become public representations that help establish norms for legitimate and acceptable individual behavior.

In the final chapter (Chapter 6), we consider some concrete economic, social, and interpersonal factors that might serve to create, perpetuate, and modify culture.

Notes

1. Durkheim, 1938.
2. Sperber, 1991.
3. Will, 1983.
4. Baron and Straus, 1989.
5. Hartz, 1969, p. 123.
6. Gelles and Cornell, 1990, p. 28; The Louisiana Slave Code of 1824, article 173, from Rose, 1976, p. 176.
7. *Jacob v. State* (1842) in 372 Tennessee 3 (1878).
8. Cited in Hart, 1992, p. 22.
9. Details are presented in Cohen, in press. Note that statistical comparisons of states are not strictly appropriate because the entire population of states has been sampled. If

the states are different, they are different, just as if the height of all men in two fraterni-
ties were measured and the average of one fraternity was to be found greater than that
of the other. We would not say the difference was "statistically significant"; we would
simply say that was the state of affairs. However, we performed statistical tests to give
some idea of the strength of the results in statistical terms. See Baron and Straus (1989)
for a discussion.

10. See Snyder, 1993; M. Anderson, 1994.

11. National Rifle Association, 1992.

12. The laws examined by the NRA involved the following: whether an application
and waiting period is required, whether a license or permit to purchase is required,
whether handguns must be registered, whether a record of the sale is sent to the state or
local government, whether states require owner licensing or ID cards, and whether
there is a state constitutional provision allowing for firearms. (The last item was reverse-
scored.)

13. Handgun Control Incorporated, no date a and no date b. For the Senate, they
identified ten key votes over the period from 1985 to 1991; for the House of Representatives they identified nine key votes from 1986 to 1991. These included votes on establishing a national waiting period for handgun purchases, allowing the continued manu-
facture of semiautomatic assault weapons made with domestic parts, and regulating the
interstate sale and transport of handguns, among other issues. An index for each legisla-
tor was constructed by assigning a 1 for every vote consistent with the HCI position (for
gun control) and a 0 for every vote against.

14. In the House, votes of western legislators on gun control issues differed significantly from votes of both southern and northern legislators, by post-hoc comparisons.

15. Gillespie, 1989, chap. 2.

16. Sloan, 1987, p. 17.

17. Mischke, 1981, p. 1001.

18. Robinson, 1984, p. 84.

19. LaFave and Scott, 1986, p. 659.

20. Laws regarding the retreat rule were examined for the case of an innocent person
assaulted outside his or her home, because all states recognize that being in one's home
at least alters, if not completely invalidates, the duty to retreat (American Law Reports
3d, 1969, p. 1297; Mischke, 1981, p. 1009). Because case law is well established in states
across the nation, it was also analyzed. Where the answer was not clear from examination of statutory and case law, lawyers at the state attorney general's office, public de-
fender's office, or other experts were called for interpretation.

21. LaFave and Scott, 1986, p. 661.

22. Means for the defense of home and property index were: North = .28, West = .45,
South = .40. $t(47) = 2.85$, $p < .01$.

23. Gilmore, 1990, pp. 19–20.

24. Barone and Ujifusa, 1991.

25. Barone and Ujifusa, 1991, pp. xix–xx.

26. Barone and Ujifusa, 1991, p. 1477

27. Barone and Ujifusa, 1991, pp. xiii–xix.

28. To reduce the possibility that these results merely reflected a general conservatism found in the South and West and not an approval of violence per se, we attempted to control for general non-defense-related conservatism (as indicated by key
votes on nondefense issues) in a regression analysis and then analyzed the residuals. The

regional effect on hawkishness was eliminated in the Senate but remained quite strong in the House. On our other foreign policy measures, the hawkishness of the South tended to remain strong even after nondefense conservatism was controlled for. The hawkishness of the West, however, was greatly diminished.

29. Gelles and Cornell, 1990, chap. 2; Gelles and Straus, 1988, pp. 31–32; Hart, 1992, p. 3.

30. Davidson, 1977, cited in Hart, 1992; Gelles and Cornell, 1990, p. 28; Gelles and Straus, 1988, p. 31.

31. Gelles and Cornell, 1990, p. 28.

32. Hart, 1992, p. 22.

33. Hart, 1992, p. 3.

34. Dobash and Dobash, 1977–1978; Bograd, 1988.

35. Daly and Wilson, 1988.

36. Hart, 1992, pp. 31–32.

37. Frazier, 1990; The Last ? Resort, 1990.

38. Flanagan and Maguire, 1992.

39. Ellsworth and Ross, 1983.

40. See Sears and Kinder, 1971; and Kinder and Sears, 1981, on symbolic racism; see also Katz, 1960.

41. Sears and Kinder, 1971, p. 66.

42. Sears and Kinder, 1971, p. 66.

43. See discussions by Ellsworth and Ross, 1983; Gross, 1993; Gross and Mauro, 1989.

44. More-extensive details on the method can be found in Cohen and Nisbett, 1995.

45. Of the 921 letters sent, 9 were returned as undeliverable and 112 responses were received, for a response rate of 12 percent. We anticipated northern companies would be relatively more likely to respond to the theft letter than to the homicide letter. That was the trend, but it fell short of significance.

46. Of the 303 letters sent out, 94 responses were received, for a response rate of 31 percent. In Figure 5.13, we present results from the 83 white respondents for the sake of consistency. However, the results look similar if the 11 nonwhite respondents are added in.

47. As expected, there were huge differences between papers of the South and West versus the North in how long reporters had lived in these regions. The correlation between the region of the paper and the region of origin of the reporter was .90 ($p < .001$). Not surprisingly then, results look very similar if we categorize by region of the reporter instead of region of the paper.

48. Triandis, 1995; Markus and Kitayama, 1991; Shweder, 1991.

6

Culture of Honor: Manifestations, Explanations, and Destinations

I$_N$ THIS CHAPTER we tie together several loose strings. First, we summarize what has been established by the evidence, and we argue that the evidence is best understood as the consequence of a culture-of-honor tradition in the South rather than of other factors that have been proposed. We examine the role of women in the southern culture of honor, including the extent to which they socialize and sanction male behavior and the extent to which they participate in a culture of honor themselves. We return to a discussion of our thesis about the frontier-herding origins of this culture of honor. And then we generalize the economic argument, considering economies and cultures that are, at least superficially, very different from that of the southern United States. Finally, we turn to the question of cultural persistence and change in order to speculate about the future of cultures of honor in the U.S. South and elsewhere.

Summarizing the Facts About Differences in Regional Violence

We believe that we have established three major points about violence and the U.S. South and those parts of the West initially settled by southerners. First, the South is indeed more violent, at least as defined by propensity to commit homicide. Second, the attitudes and behaviors of individual southerners are such as to justify violence under a specified set of conditions. Third, various public representations, including laws, institutions, and social policies, are expressive of values justifying violence under many of those same conditions.

Homicide and the South

It seems clear that the South has a higher level of the most extreme form of violence, namely, homicide. That is true at every size of population unit from the

81

state to the smallest county. This discovery is not a new one, but it has been necessary to reestablish it because of the large literature based on highly aggregated data sets that make no distinctions between black and white homicide or among population units of different size. We found that regional differences, as would be expected by our culture-of-honor hypothesis, were obtained only for whites and not for blacks, whose culture was not expected to vary in this way by region. We also found that the smaller the population unit, the stronger the regional differences were, a pattern that would be expected if the origins of regional differences were agricultural. The higher homicide rate of the South is not attributable to the South's having more guns per capita. A good "control" for this point is the fact that gun ownership is equally common in the most rural areas of the South and central Midwest, but homicide rates in the white population of those areas differ by a factor of four.

Attitudes and Behaviors Relating to the Culture of Honor

The pattern of attitudes and behaviors that we have described is a quite specific one, consistent with the hypothesis that the South retains a version of the culture of honor—that is, a culture in which protection of a reputation for toughness is highly important and in which insults cannot be tolerated.

1. The only types of homicide that are more frequent in the South are those in which affronts and threats to property or integrity of self are likely to be involved—arguments, brawls, and lovers' triangles.
2. Southerners do not approve of violence in the abstract, nor do they approve of violence for any concrete purposes that we have been able to discover—except for protection of self, family, and possessions, for responding to an insult, and for socializing children. Southerners may favor violence for purposes of social control, but we attribute that to the experience of slavery rather than to the culture of honor.
3. Our laboratory studies of southern college students show that when they are insulted, they manifest a range of physiological, cognitive, and behavioral reactions that distinguish them from southerners who are not insulted and from northerners, whether insulted or not.
   a. Insulted southerners are more stressed, as indicated by the increases they show in cortisol level.
   b. They are more prepared for aggression, as indicated by the increases they show in testosterone level.
   c. They are more "primed" to consider violent solutions to situations involving an insult, as indicated by the completions they wrote for scenarios beginning with an affront.
   d. They display more anger and less amusement (under at least some circumstances).

e. They display more aggression in our version of the "chicken" game, moving aside at a very late point to allow our 6-foot-3-inch, 250-pound confederate to pass.

f. They engage in more dominance behavior, as rated by an observer with whom they interact briefly.

Public Representations

The culture of honor appears to be sustained by collective manifestations ranging from shared assumptions about the beliefs of others to institutional codes including laws and social policies. In our laboratory work, we found that southerners believe that a person who has observed them being insulted will think they are weak and not masculine. Hence, the southerner's tacit representation of the "generalized other" includes the notion that failure to respond to insulting behavior will be met with contempt.

A variety of laws, institutions, and social policies requiring the participation of many people in a shared meaning system is consistent with the culture-of-honor characterization of the South. These include opposition to gun control; a preference for laws allowing for violence in protection of self, home, and property; a preference for a strong national defense; a preference for the institutional use of violence in socializing children; and a willingness to carry out capital punishment and other forms of state violence for preventing crime and maintaining social order. In addition, individuals acting in their institutional roles—in our studies, as employers and newspaper reporters—are more forgiving of honor-related violence and are more inclined to see such violence as justified by the provocation of another.

Alternative Explanations for Violence

We favor explaining the violence of the South as a manifestation of a culture of honor, with some specific forms of violence in the Old South additionally related to the experience with slavery. But what of the role of other explanations that have been offered (and accepted by many thoughtful observers) for decades or even centuries? There are three main classes of explanation.

Temperature

It has long been assumed that tempers flare when the temperature is high and that violence is often the consequence. There is evidence that this assumption is true. Several investigators have shown that violent crimes are more likely when temperatures are higher.[1] Nonlethal violent acts such as "accidents" in professional baseball are also more common on hot days than on cool ones.[2] Although this evidence makes one suspect that temperature may play a role in the greater violence of the South, there are several reasons to believe that temperature is not a very significant factor in producing the homicide differences we have demonstrated:

1. The magnitude of homicide differences between regions is completely incommensurate with the commonly observed effect of temperature on violent crime. There is less than a 20 percent difference in violent crime rate between the three coolest quarters of the year and the hottest quarter.[3] Even the very hottest few days of the year—above 100°F (38°C)—are associated with only a doubling in violent crime rates.[4] In contrast, the differences between South and North—*averaged over the entire year*—range up to a factor of four, depending on the size of the population unit studied.
2. The temperature hypothesis could not explain why regional differences range from very slight, for big cities, to very great, for the smallest, most rural counties. Georgia's villages are warmer than those of Massachusetts, and the homicide rate is far greater in Georgia's villages than in those of Massachusetts. But Georgia's big cities are also warmer than those of Massachusetts and there is little regional homicide difference for big cities. Temperature could scarcely account for this pattern.
3. A similar conclusion can be reached by comparing black and white homicide rates. It is only white rates that differ by region, not black ones.
4. The temperature hypothesis is contradicted by the pattern of homicide differences observed within the South. Homicide rates are higher in the relatively cool mountainous regions of the South than in the relatively hot moist plains regions.

Poverty

Within developed nations, poverty is a good predictor of homicide.[5] Just why this should be the case is not obvious, but it is an empirical fact that must be dealt with because the South as a whole is poorer than the rest of the nation. Once again, however, we do not believe regional differences in rates of poverty can possibly explain the specific pattern of results presented here. This is true for several reasons:

1. Regional differences in white homicide rate survive regression analyses that include poverty as a factor. In fact, regional differences are *magnified* for the largest cities when poverty is controlled for.
2. In the small rural counties we studied, there were no income differences between North and South, yet there are very big homicide rate differences in rural counties.

3. *Within* the South, the rural regions that Reaves and Nisbett studied differ relatively little in income but differ greatly in homicide rate.
4. Though there are some slight attitude differences toward violence that are associated with income, as well as with education and age, those differences do not show the same pattern as do the attitude differences associated with region.
5. We found dramatic differences in the reactions of southern and northern University of Michigan students to an insult, despite the fact that on average the southern students were not poor by any definition and came from families that were actually somewhat better off financially than those of northern students.

Slavery

Through the centuries, the preferred explanation of the source of southern violence has been the institution of slavery: It has been argued that whites used corporal punishment to control their slaves and that they generalized this behavior to whites in their environment. We think it is entirely likely that there is some merit to this explanation. In fact, we have shown that there is a preference in the slave South for violence as a means of achieving social control—ranging from corporal punishment in the schools to capital punishment for murderers—that is not shared with the West or even the nonslave South, which are otherwise similar to the slave South in attitudes and behaviors relating to violence. It therefore remains quite plausible that the southern support for violence for social control is the result of the historical legacy of slavery. But there are several reasons for doubting that the South's greater preference for violence is due *entirely* to slavery.

1. Within the South, it is the regions where slavery was common that have the *lowest* homicide rates.
2. The West, which shares highly elevated homicide rates with the South, has no history of slavery.
3. Most of the attitudes that we characterize as deriving from a culture of honor do not seem to derive in any direct way from a tradition of slavery. If slavery leads to greater acceptability of violence, why not violence as a solution to problems in general rather than the quite specific situations that characterize southern preference for violence?

We do not wish to deny that temperature, poverty, and slavery may be factors contributing to violence. However, we think the best and most comprehensive single explanation for violence in the South is its history as a culture of honor.

The Role of Women in the Culture of Honor

It might seem strange that we have systematically excluded half of the southern white population—women—from our study of the culture of honor. This is due in part to the fact that men are overwhelmingly responsible for most homicides and acts of violence in this country and throughout the world.[6] More important, research on the culture of honor is overwhelmingly about men, because men in such cultures live and breathe and act out the requirements of the culture of honor in the most visible and consequential ways. Much of the "mystique" of the culture of honor is tied in explicit ways to concepts of manhood. Who a man is in such cultures has everything to do with how much of a man he is—defined in terms of toughness and respect. Nevertheless, women are clearly very much a part of all cultures of honor—teaching it to their sons, enforcing it on their menfolk, and, quite often, even participating in its violent behavior patterns themselves. This was true historically and it appears to be true in many cultures of honor today.

Women's Role in Socialization

The warriors of ancient Greece and Sparta fought with swords and shields. If they ran from a battle, they would cast away their shields in order to carry less weight in flight. If killed in battle, they were brought home lying on their shields. When the Spartan mother sent her son to war, she is supposed to have exhorted him to return "with his shield or upon it." The historian Bertram Wyatt-Brown has written of the Old South's admiration for this attitude: "No encomium to Southern womankind was complete without a reminder of Sparta's brave mothers."[7] And women of the southern highlands did not "shrink from the suffering and sacrifice involved [in feuds], but rather [would] excite and cheer their husbands to desperate deeds. They would hate a man who took insult or injury without revenge."[8]

Both Andrew Jackson's mother and Sam Houston's mother were women of the Tennessee Highlands. Jackson's mother is said to have told him: "Never tell a lie, nor take what is not your own, nor sue anybody for slander or assault and battery. *Always settle them cases yourself!*"[9] Jackson appears to have followed his mother's advice: He was involved in over a hundred documented violent quarrels, including several duels, in one of which he killed a man. Houston recalled his mother saying, on the occasion of giving him a musket for use in the army: "'Never disgrace it; for remember, I had rather all my sons should fill one honorable grave, than that one of them should turn his back to save his life.' She then gave him a plain gold ring with the word 'Honor' engraved inside it."[10]

An old veteran of the Civil War was once asked why southern soldiers had fought so bravely and so long after it had become apparent that they would be crushed by the North. "We were afraid to stop. . . . Afraid of the women at home. . . . They would have been ashamed of us."[11]

Women's Active Participation in the Culture of Honor

It is clear that in many societies females not only prepare their male children for the culture of honor and enforce it on their menfolk: They participate in it themselves. In some Mediterranean cultures, it is the women who routinely carry out some sorts of homicides, for example, the stoning to death of women believed to be unfaithful. In others, it is understood that if there is no man available to carry out a homicide, a woman must do it. (Sometimes she does so dressed in a man's clothing.)

The female Celtic forebears of the Scotch-Irish in the South were regarded as ferocious fighters by the Romans.

> A whole troupe of foreigners would not be able to withstand a single Gaul if he called his wife to his assistance who is usually very strong and with blue eyes; especially when, swelling her neck, gnashing her teeth, and brandishing her sallow arms of enormous size, she begins to strike blows mingled with kicks, as if they were so many missiles sent from the string of a catapult.[12]

The stereotype of the southern female is that she was highly feminine. Though there may be some truth to that stereotype, there is a competing one, that she was a "steel magnolia," a superficially soft and melting woman who was quite capable of toughness and the wielding of power. Historically, the socialization of southern girls was, early in life at least, not too different from that of boys.

> Very young children learned that they were supposed to grab for things, fight on the carpet to entertain parents, clatter their toys about, defy parental commands, and even set upon likely visitors in friendly roughhouse. Girls acted with the same freedom from restraint as boys. Their introduction to the proprieties of ladyhood came much later.[13]

Whatever plantation women may have been like, it is clear from all sorts of evidence that in the backcountry, women were very tough indeed. In fact, some of the most violent backcountry bandits were women.[14]

We have evidence in our own data of the strong role played by contemporary southern women in the culture of honor.

1. In examining homicide data, we find that white southern women are much more likely to kill than their northern counterparts. That is particularly true when the circumstances involve a lovers' triangle, brawl, or argument. White southern *men* account for a disproportionate 41 percent of *all* white male–perpetrated homicides and an especially high percent of all lovers' triangle homicides (49 percent), alcohol brawl–related homicides (66 percent), and argument-related homicides (40 percent). Meanwhile, white southern *women* account for 48 percent of *all* white female–perpetrated homicides and an even

more disproportionate percent of all lovers' triangle (55 percent), alcohol brawl–related (72 percent), and argument-related homicides (52 percent).

Since many female-perpetrated homicides are in response to violence by a partner, it is unclear whether the higher rate of white southern female homicides (1) is simply a reaction to more violent southern men or (2) reflects a lower threshold for what southern women will "tolerate" from their men before becoming violent. One would guess that both possibilities have some truth to them. In any case, we know that the ratio of wives who kill husbands (relative to husbands who kill wives) is disproportionately high in the South. That is, for white offenders, 45 percent of all husband-kills-wife homicides occurred in the South, and an even higher proportion—58 percent—of all wife-kills-husband homicides occurred in the South.

2. Our attitude data show that southern women, like southern men, are more likely than their northern counterparts to endorse violence for answering an affront, to oppose gun control, and to support spanking. And the gap between southern women and northern women is at least as big as the gap between southern men and northern men on these dimensions.

3. No female subjects participated in our experiments, but in one of our studies we did ask about the regional background of the subjects' parents. The number of cases was small, but it seemed that having a mother from the South was important in producing the "southern" response to our insult—and indeed, having a mother from the South seemed to be a better predictor of the "southern response" than having a father from the South.

4. Finally, the southern ideology of violence seems to be shared by women elites. Female members of the U.S. House of Representatives from the South were more likely to advocate a strong military and be against gun control than their northern counterparts. (There were not enough female senators to make meaningful comparisons.)

In short, it seems that southern women are active in the culture of honor, just as their men are. It is probably no accident that the first state to be governed by women—having at one point a female governor, U.S. senator, mayors of five of the largest seven cities, and chief of police of its largest city—was a southern state, namely Texas. In that state, as former Governor Ann Richards put it, "Everyone has to prove their masculinity—especially women!"

The Psycho-Economic Roots
of the Culture of Honor

Although we think we have established that there was and is a culture of honor in the South, the weakest part of our thesis concerns the origins of this culture of honor. It is much harder to prove where a culture comes from than to show that it exists. Nevertheless, we believe that our frontier-herding hypothesis is well grounded in the work of anthropologists, evolutionary psychologists, historians, and sociologists.

We believe the southern culture of honor derives from the herding economy brought to the region by the earliest settlers and practiced by them for many decades thereafter. This assertion hinges primarily on the apparent association between herding economies and cultures of honor worldwide and on the conjecture that the herding economy and violence are related because of the inherent risks involved in such an economy. The herdsman continually faces the possibility of losing his animals through the actions of others. The issue of protection is therefore a very serious one, and the herdsman cultivates an acquaintance with violence and weapons to deter those who would prey on him. The sensitivity to insult is secondary: Its purpose is to preserve the individual's reputation for being willing and able to carry out violence if needed.

If this account of the origins of the culture of honor is correct, that would have an important implication, which is that cultures of honor should not be limited to herding economies. Such cultures should be found wherever the possibility exists that scarcity will be produced by the predatory actions of others, especially when the state is unwilling or unable to provide protection from such predation.

Economies Producing Forces Against the Culture of Honor

Our hypothesis suggests that cultures of honor should be relatively rare for some kinds of economies, particularly, hunter-gatherer economies and stable agricultural economies.[15] Hunter-gatherer economies rarely have a large enough surplus for another group of hunter-gatherers to be willing to risk death to obtain it. And in any case, the energy of a hunter-gatherer would be better expended in finding food for himself than in trying to take the meager portion of another hunter-gatherer.[16] Farmers in stable agricultural communities have a greater investment in remaining peacefully on their land than in stealing their neighbor's surplus. Moreover, farmers usually have granaries that provide enough surplus for them to survive a number of poor harvests in a row. They would literally have to be starving to make it rational to steal bread from their neighbors—with whom peaceful coexistence is essential to productive economic activity. In addition, the very stability of such societies often supports a state powerful enough to protect against theft and raiding. (Of course, the agriculturalist is often at risk from the mounted or seafaring plunderer, as was the case in China, Europe, and the Middle East for centuries. Various solutions to this problem, ranging from the Great Wall to a standing army with the specialized task of defense, have been attempted, but conversion of an entire agrarian society to a warrior-like, honor-based culture seems to be rare.)

Slash-and-Burn Farming and the Utility of the Raid

One type of economy that often does fit both criteria, frequent scarcity and weakness of the state, is slash-and-burn farming, or horticulture. Many parts of the world have soil of such low productivity that improvements to it in the form of fertilizer or allowing it to lie fallow for brief periods are not efficient. The most effective way to subsist is to clear the land, use it for three or four years until it is no longer productive, and move on to some other site.

If that means of production were always successful, there would be no need to try to steal the output of other people, but it is not always successful. In parts of the world where slash-and-burn farming tends to be the only practical agriculture—for example, in Central and South American rain forests, the Indonesian rain forest, and parts of West Africa—it is common for temperature and precipitation to vary over a wide range. If the weather is too hot and dry or too wet, there may be a very poor harvest. Even if calories are sufficient, sources of protein may be in short supply. But one's neighbor may well have enough food stored—because of the local terrain, or greater industry, or better luck—to make a raid a reasonable cost-benefit proposition. Because of the "portability" of such societies and the rain forest impenetrability, there is rarely a state with enough strength to prevent such raids. Both warfare and internal violence are characteristic of at least some such societies. Examples include the Yanamamo of Central South America, many groups in Southeast Asia, and the headhunters of the Philippines.[17] Many of these societies are accurately characterized as having typical cultures of honor in which warrior prowess is prized above all for males and threats to reputation are treated with utmost seriousness. (It should be noted, however, that the claim is often made for some of these groups that the aggression is not in the service of obtaining food but for purposes of obtaining women.)

The Inner City and the Culture of Honor

In May 1994, a 65-year-old plumber named James Todd accidentally bumped into a teenager in a store in Brooklyn. He apparently failed to say "excuse me" or failed to say it fast enough or in an appropriate tone of voice. According to a witness, the boy felt "dissed" (shown disrespect). An argument resulted and after Todd left the store, "the teenager caught up to him on a bicycle, pulled out a gun and shot him point blank in the head. Mr. Todd died instantly."[18]

Similar cases, where young people fight and die over what would seem to be "petty" affronts, are not rare. Especially in the inner cities, respect is a commodity that many deem worth dying for, as the sociologist Elijah Anderson observed about the "code of the streets."

> At the heart of the code is the issue of respect—loosely defined as being treated "right," or granted the deference one deserves. . . . In the street culture, especially among young people, respect is viewed as almost an external entity that is hard-won but easily lost, and so must constantly be guarded. The rules of the code in fact provide a framework for negotiating respect. The person whose very appearance—including his clothing, demeanor, and way of moving—deters transgressions feels that he possesses, and may be considered by others to possess, a mea-

sure of respect. With the right amount of respect, for instance, he can avoid "being bothered" in public. If he is bothered, not only may he be in physical danger but he has been disgraced or "dissed."[19]

Anderson's explanation of this syndrome—which the reader will easily recognize as a type of culture of honor—seems in harmony with the general explanation we have put forward for the existence of such cultures. There is a scarcity of economic resources in the inner city owing to unemployment, which is produced by factors ranging from racism to loss of manufacturing jobs. This creates a situation where theft and other illegal activities are rewarded more than the alternatives and, thus, to a situation where citizens need to be vigilant in their own protection.

The state contributes to this skewed payoff structure by its neglect. "Gun owners like to say, 'Call for a cop, call for an ambulance, and call for a pizza. See which comes first.' "[20] As the rap group Public Enemy noted in the title of its hit song, "911 Is a Joke" in many inner city neighborhoods. The implications for having to defend oneself and for establishing a code of honor are clear. Thus, it may be reasonable that a "lack of police accountability has in fact been incorporated into the status system: the person who is believed capable of 'taking care of himself' is accorded a certain deference, which translates into a sense of physical and psychological control."[21]

Children learn the lessons of the culture of honor early:

Even small children test one another, pushing and shoving, and are ready to hit other children over circumstances not to their liking. In turn, they are readily hit by other children, and the child who is toughest prevails. . . . The child in effect is initiated into a system that is really a way of campaigning for respect. . . . Those street-oriented adults with whom children come in contact . . . help them along in forming this understanding by verbalizing the messages they are getting through experience: . . . "Protect yourself." "Don't punk out." "If you don't whup his ass, I'll whup your ass when you come home."[22]

In the presence of scarcity, high potential gain from theft and illegal activities, and low probability of state protection, the culture of honor has been reinvented yet another time in human history. Thus, in our view, the United States has at least one major group other than white rural southerners—namely, members of the "street" subculture of the inner city—that is well characterized as a culture of honor. Along with Elijah Anderson, William Julius Wilson, and other observers, we believe the fundamental explanation for the existence of this subculture is economic. If so, the culture of the inner city is not likely to change until the economic situation changes. If then. In the next and final section of this chapter, we examine questions of cultural evolution and persistence. It is an open question whether economic change is always—or at any rate rapidly—accompanied by cultural change.

Future Directions for
Contemporary Cultures of Honor

It seems clear that the culture of honor of the South no longer has the strength it once had. Men no longer fight with "no holds barred." Feuding is in disrepute even in the most remote areas of the backcountry, mountain South. So will the culture of honor of the southern United States wither to the point that the society will be indistinguishable from that of the North?

It might seem that the answer is obviously yes. Few people depend on herding for their livelihood any longer, and those who do are well protected by the state. In the absence of compelling economic factors, the culture of honor might appear doomed.

Functional Autonomy and Pluralistic Ignorance

Cultures, however, do not necessarily respond only to material or objective conditions. There are several reasons why the culture of honor of the South might retain some force indefinitely.

Southern subjects in our experiment assumed that an observer who had seen them get insulted would think ill of them—regarding them as less tough and masculine. Such a belief indicates that southerners think that a failure to take action against insults will be met with loss of respect. If they believe that, they could be expected to be more likely to take action when insulted than northerners, who do not expect disapproval. Taking action against insults often will be observed by others, who in turn have their "honor" norms reinforced, as well as their assumptions that failure to abide by them would result in further disapproval. In other words, there could be a case of pure "functional autonomy"[23] for some aspects of the culture of honor. There is no longer any economic reason for southern males to show their physical toughness, yet they believe they will suffer social loss if they do not. For individuals, it may be *socially* beneficial to continue with culture-of-honor norms, and the norms may be upheld for that reason. Hence, the culture could keep some of its properties indefinitely even in the absence of any material or rational reasons for retaining those properties, because "being a man" entails readiness for violence.

An ironic variant on this functional autonomy theory concerns the possibility that southerners are operating in a state of "pluralistic ignorance"[24] in which most individuals are mistaken about the real views of other group members. It could be the case that the personal attitudes of most southerners have moved away from the presumed norms but that opportunities to discover that change are limited. For example, it seems quite possible that our southern college subjects might have been mistaken in believing that an observer would think badly of them for failing to retaliate. A real southern observer might, on the contrary, not think ill of a person who refused to retaliate when insulted. To disabuse people of a false belief about norms would require feedback to the effect that the community regards taking offense at an insult or responding to it aggressively as undesirable. Such feedback may be rare enough that members of a culture believe that the norm is still shared. That may result in what Miller and Prentice call a "conservative lag," in which public norms lag behind private attitudes: "Social practices will stay in place long after they have lost private support because people do not recognize that their personal shift in attitude is shared by others."[25]

Manhood and Honor

The factors just described may be part of the reason the culture has remained even after economic circumstances have changed. Tied up with these issues is the problem that the culture of honor was always a culture of *honor* and not just a culture of *deterrence.* That is, although the economic circumstances may have made the culture a functional adaptation, the culture of honor is not exclusively built on economic rationales, certainly not on conscious ones. In cultures of honor, men are expected to lay themselves on the line for noble causes—duty, honor, family.

As David Gilmore observed in his book *Manhood in the Making,* cultures of honor build their codes of conduct into definitions of what it means to be a man. The world over, men are sent out to sacrifice and to die, not for such purely instrumental purposes as deterrence; rather they are motivated by what they and the community expect good, honorable men to do. Thus, the ideals of the culture of honor are built into one's social identity and may become divorced from ideas about economic survival.

Once those ideals are separated from the initial reasons for their existence and incorporated into gender roles, they may become much more impervious to change. Many patterns of behavior continue because they are defined as things that *a man just does:* he protects his family from threats, he answers serious insults with violence, he spanks his children to discipline them, and he protects his honor and status in the community. Reasons are irrelevant. Those are just things you have to do.

As John Reed has written:

> How do southerners learn that violence is acceptable in some circumstances, but not others? This aspect of culture, I suggest, is simply taken in like others. Like the words to 'Blessed Assurance,' the technique of the yo-yo, or the conviction that okra is edible, it is absorbed, pretty much without reflection, in childhood. . . . [As a schoolboy], if you were called out for some offense, you fought. I guess you could have appealed to the teacher, but that just—wasn't done. And that phrase speaks volumes.[26]

Because culture is taken in without reflection, because we acquire it more by *absorbing* it than by studying it, the ultimate reason for why we do things (or why a behavior is functional) is often hidden from us. We do not reexamine cultural rules every generation or analyze how functionally adaptive they are before we internalize them. So, as long as they do not get us in too much trouble in some way that is manifest and as long as there is no far more attractive alternative, they will continue. Indeed, as long as there is social enforcement of the norms, it may be profitable to continue to behave in accord with such norms and costly to defy them even when one consciously, personally rejects them.

An important implication of that analysis is that one should speculate not merely on whether the culture of honor will wither when material circumstances cease to make it rational but also on whether the culture could maintain itself, or even grow, for nonmaterial reasons. We have speculated about some nonmaterial factors that could keep a given cultural stance alive indefinitely, but other nonmaterial circumstances could cause its spread. In the terms of Dan Sperber's "epidemiology of representations" notion, humans probably have substantial "susceptibility" to the culture-of-honor stance.[27] There is a romance and an allure to the Masai warrior, the Druze tribesman, the Sioux Indian, the Scottish chieftain, an allure to which few people are utterly immune. It seems possible that gangs, inner-city-type, which currently seem to be springing up even among white youth in the northern heartland, represent a response to the allure of the stance among those who have little to gain by playing by society's rules and little to lose by standing outside of them.

Another implication has to do with attempts at deliberate social change. The more deeply rooted a given stance is in social norms, definitions of gender role, and personal identity, the harder it will be to change. There is great concern with violence in our society today, and much effort is being put into providing young people with "conflict resolution skills." Though such programs may have some value, this book should have made it clear that in some subcultures, conflict is not something to resolve but rather something that one is required to confront or even generate. From that perspective, intervention programs that show individuals that they are living in a state of pluralistic ignorance with regard to disapproval of nonviolent behavior, or programs that teach ways to get community respect without resort to violence, seem more likely to succeed with some groups.

This final section of the book has been by far the most speculative, and yet the issues are among the most theoretically fascinating and pragmatically important. Questions of cultural evolution and change, together with even more fundamental questions about the reciprocal relation between individual behavior and public representation, seem likely to occupy center stage in the emerging field of cultural psychology.

Notes

1. Anderson, 1987, 1989; Cotton, 1986; Rotton and Frey, 1985.
2. Reifman, Larrick, and Fein, 1991.
3. Anderson, 1987.

4. Harries and Stadler, 1988.

5. Siegel, 1989.

6. Daly and Wilson, 1988.

7. Wyatt-Brown, 1982, p. 93.

8. Hatcher, 1934, p. 391.

9. McWhiney, 1988, pp. 169–170, italics in original.

10. Houston, cited in Wyatt-Brown, 1982.

11. E. B. Kennon, cited in Wyatt-Brown, 1982, p. 172.

12. Ammianus Marcellinus, cited in Chadwick, 1970, p. 50.

13. Wyatt-Brown, 1982, p. 138.

14. Fischer, 1989, p. 772.

15. O'Kelley and Carney, 1986.

16. This is not to say that homicide rates are low among hunter-gatherers; they may not be (Daly and Wilson, 1988). But hunter-gatherer cultures do not exhibit the characteristics of cultures of honor.

17. Chagnon, 1966, 1968, 1974, 1992; Rosaldo, M. Z., 1980; Rosaldo, R., 1980.

18. Pearson, 1994, p. A17.

19. E. Anderson, 1994, p. 82.

20. Will, 1993, p. 94.

21. E. Anderson, 1994, p. 82.

22. E. Anderson, 1994, p. 86.

23. Allport, 1937.

24. Allport, 1924; Katz and Allport, 1931.

25. Miller and Prentice, 1994, p. 543.

26. Reed, 1981, p. 13.

27. Sperber, 1991.

Appendix A

Southernness Index. We used Gastil's index of southernness,[1] based on the degree to which the state was initially settled by southerners, as the indicator of southernness. States of the Confederate South (except Florida) receive a value of 30 in the index; states such as Oklahoma, with populations that initially were overwhelmingly from the South, receive a 25; those such as Colorado, with populations about half from the South at the time of settlement, receive a 20; and so on, down to those such as the New England states, with very little Southern population at any time, which receive a 5. Gastil's index has been criticized on several grounds, mainly because it rests on early immigration data rather than more-contemporary data on the percent in the state of southern birth. The Gastil index and percent of the current population born in the South are, however, correlated beyond the .90 level,[2] so there seems to be no reason not to employ the more frequently used Gastil index.

Poverty Index. Our poverty index was composed of five different variables, all of which have been used by other investigators, drawn from the 1980 U.S. Census. The variables, which were transformed to standard scores and weighted equally, were the following: (1) percent of persons in the city below the poverty line, (2) percent of households on public assistance, (3) percent of persons over 25 years old with less than five years of education, (4) percent of children living in one-parent homes, and (5) adult unemployment rate. Unfortunately, the census does not break down these data into racial and ethnic categories for all smaller cities. Thus, we analyzed the data both for all cities in the sample and for just those cities that are 90 percent or more white and non-Hispanic. (However, no city of 200,000 or more persons has a population 90 percent or more non-Hispanic whites.)

GINI Index. Our index of economic inequality was based on Adams's technique,[3] which can be used to assess this variable for communities of relatively small size as well as for cities of larger size.

Density. Density, or number of people per square mile in 1980, was obtained from the *County and City Data Book.*[4]

Percent of Males Age 15–29 in the White Non-Hispanic Population in 1980. This variable was obtained from the National Planning Data Corporation, Ithaca, N.Y., using the U.S. Census.

Notes

1. Gastil, 1971.
2. Huff-Corzine, Corzine, and Moore, 1986.
3. Adams, 1991.
4. U.S. Bureau of the Census, 1983.

TABLE A.1 Bivariate Correlations Between Homicide Rates and Predictor Variables for Cities of Size 50,000 or More

	1	2	3	4	5	6	7	8	9
1 Male offender									
2 Victim	.97***								
3 GINI index	.44***	.40***							
4 Density	.31***	.31***	.06						
5 Poverty index	.73***	.72***	.55***	.47***					
6 % males 15–29	–.11	–.12	.17	–.15*	–.02				
7 Southernness index	.40***	.35***	.29***	–.28***	.16**	.14*			
8 Population	.35***	.35***	.13	.50***	.26***	–.06	–.03		
9 % black	.79***	.78***	.38***	.29***	.74***	–.05	.40***	.19**	

N of cities = 211

* significant at .05 level
** significant at .01 level
*** significant at .001 level

TABLE A.2   Regression Coefficients for Homicide Rates in Cities of Size 50,000 or More

Variable	Standardized Coefficient	Unstandardized Coefficient	Standard Error	t value
	Male Offender Rate			
GINI index	.044	.195	.208	.937
Density	−.044	.000	.000	−.867
Poverty index	.312	1.100	.242	4.535***
% males 15–29	−.109	−.473	.163	−2.908**
Southernness index	.160	.252	.072	3.497***
Population	.203	.000	.000	4.817***
% black	.449	.355	.048	7.336***
Adjusted R² = .74				
	Victim Rate			
GINI index	−.009	−.030	.159	−.187
Density	−.062	.000	.000	−1.129
Poverty index	.352	.889	.184	4.819***
% males 15–29	−.105	−.329	.124	−2.652**
Southernness index	.128	.145	.055	2.628**
Population	.206	.000	.000	4.594***
% black	.439	.249	.037	6.742***
Adjusted R² = .70				

N of cities = 211
  * significant at .05 level
  ** significant at .01 level
  *** significant at .001 level

TABLE A.3   Correlations and Standardized Regression Coefficients Relating Southernness and Homicide Rates for Whites and Blacks as a Function of City Size (regression coefficients in parentheses)

	Whites		Blacks	
City Size	Male Offender Rate	Victim Rate	Male Offender Rate	Victim Rate
10–50,000	.37***	.42***	.35***	.14
	(.20)**	(.23)**	(.21)*	(.11)
50–200,000	.40***	.39***	.10	.06
	(.32)***	(.31)***	(.14)	(−.02)
>200,000	.10	.06	−.03	.02
	(.29)*	(.28)†	(.05)	(.14)

†p < .10
*p < .05
**p < .01
***p < .001

TABLE A.4   Standardized Regression Coefficients for White Non-Hispanic Homicide Rates for Cities that Are 90 Percent or More White and Non-Hispanic

	City Size			
	10–50,000		50–200,000	
	Male Offender Rate	Victim Rate	Male Offender Rate	Victim Rate
GINI index	−.03	.15	.26*	.14
Density	−.05	−.08	−.11	−.14
Poverty index	.38***	.25*	.42***	.46***
% males 15–29	−.10	−.06	−.22*	−.20*
Southernness index	.37***	.43***	.52**	.64**
R²	.29	.33	.49	.57

Notes: N of cities of size 10,000–50,000 = 101; N of cities of size 50,000–200,000 = 60. There are no cities of 200,000 or more that are 90 percent or more non-Hispanic whites.
*p ≤ .05
**p ≤ .01
***p ≤ .001

Appendix B

Blumenthal et al., 1972

Respondents in the Blumenthal et al. survey were "aged 16 through 64 living in the conterminous United States. . . . There were 1,374 respondents interviewed, with a structured interview schedule yielding an overall response rate of 80 percent."[1] The primary goal of the study was to understand how American men see violence when it is used for social control and social change, but questions ranged widely over issues of violence by individuals, gangs of hoodlums, and government agents.

We selected only the white respondents for these analyses. (The survey did not ask whether or not respondents were Hispanic, so we filtered on the race variable, which divided respondents into white, black, and "other".) We combined 79 white respondents from the border South (Kentucky, Maryland, Oklahoma, Tennessee, and Washington, D.C.) and 226 white respondents from the deep South (Alabama, Arkansas, Florida, Georgia, Louisiana, Mississippi, North Carolina, South Carolina, Texas, and Virginia) to create our southern category. In our nonsouthern category, there were 741 white respondents from all other regions of the country. By recent census classifications, Delaware and West Virginia would be considered southern states. However, their classification is probably irrelevant, since none of the primary sampling units used in this survey were located in these two states.

General Social Survey of NORC

The number of respondents in the surveys varied from question to question, but for most there were approximately 6,000 white male respondents. Approximately 2,000 came from the South, defined as census divisions 5, 6, and 7. Approximately 4,000 came from all other regions of the country. We report all of the survey questions having to do with ideologies about interpersonal violence that were asked in the period 1972–1990. To select out white males, we used NORC's race variable, which separated respondents into white, black, and "other." We ran analyses both including and excluding respondents who might be considered Hispanic based on their answers to questions about country of origin of their ancestors. Results were virtually identical for every item analyzed. Because there was a fair amount of uncodable data on the ethnicity question, however, we chose to use analyses filtered on the race variable only.

Rural County Survey

Respondents came from counties of under 20,000 households that were not adjacent to a metropolitan area. Every household with a listed phone number in these regions was eligible to be called and to receive a letter requesting their participation in our survey. Using Kish selection tables,[2] we randomly selected one of the males 16 years or older in the household to be interviewed. Response rate for potential respondents was about 80 percent. The survey took approximately forty minutes to administer and included a number of other questions about demographics and attitudes not related to approval of violence. Only non-Hispanic white respondents were included in the analyses in Chapter 3.

Notes

1. Blumenthal et al., 1972, p. 16.
2. Kish, 1965.

Appendix C

Questionnaires in Experiment 3 showed that except for the fact that southerners were an inch taller than northerners on average, there were no significant differences between students from the two regions—at any rate not in religious preferences, frequency of church attendance, fraternity membership, military service of their parents, status level of parents' occupations, level of parents' education, marital status of parents either at the time of subjects' participation in the experiment or when they were growing up, number of brothers or sisters, school in the university in which they were enrolled, SAT or ACT scores, or high school grade point average.

So that all students would be equated at least with respect to whether they had "self-selected" to attend school in another state, all subjects were non-Michigan residents. Jewish students were excluded because we guessed that Jewish culture might dilute regional differences. It should be noted, however, that some researchers have different intuitions on this matter.[1]

Subjects were recruited by phone and paid for their time ($5 in Experiment 1, $10 in Experiment 2, and $15 in Experiment 3, as the supply of southern students dwindled). Students who had lived in the South for a period of at least six years were considered southern, though most subjects classified as southern had lived in the South much longer—over 80 percent of their lives on average. The South was defined as census divisions 5, 6, and 7—South Atlantic, East South Central, West South Central—though that definition was altered slightly in Experiments 2 and 3. In Experiments 2 and 3, we changed the definition so that the South could be described by its "cultural geography."[2] Thus, in Experiments 2 and 3, the South was defined as states having a southernness index of 25 or more.[3] The list of states with a southernness index of 25 or more is essentially the same as that of census divisions 5, 6, and 7, except that Maryland and Delaware do not have index scores of 25 or more, whereas Arizona and New Mexico do. To increase our southern sample size, we considered Missouri and Nevada southern in Experiment 2 and considered Missouri, Nevada, Kansas, Colorado, and Maryland southern in Experiment 3, since those are states that border on the South or Southwest and have southernness indices of 20, indicating that they were settled substantially by southerners. Expanding the definition of southerner was necessary to get enough subjects, but it should also be added that relaxing the criteria for southernness would generally work against our hypothesis. In these experiments, students from Washington, D.C., and from towns we could identify as its immediate suburbs were excluded, since D.C. is probably not representative of either northern or southern culture. All other students were considered northern. They had spent only about 5 percent of their lives in the South on average.

Notes

1. See Fischer, 1989, p. 874.
2. Zelinsky, 1973.
3. From Gastil, 1971.

References

Adams, T. K. (1991). *Calculation of GINI index for low-population areas of the U.S.* (Technical Report). Ann Arbor: University of Michigan, Institute for Social Research.

Allport, F. H. (1924). *Social Psychology.* Boston: Houghton Mifflin.

Allport, G. W. (1937). *Personality: A psychological interpretation.* London: Constable and Company.

American Law Reports III (1969). *Homicide: Duty to retreat where assailant and assailed share the same living quarters* 26, 1296–1307.

Ammerman, D. (1989). Revolutionary era. In Wilson and Ferris (1989).

Anderson, C. A. (1987). Temperature and aggression: Effects on quarterly, yearly, and city rates of violent and nonviolent crime. *Journal of Personality and Social Psychology* 52, 1161–1173.

_____ (1989). Temperature and aggression: Ubiquitous effects of heat on occurrence of human violence. *Psychological Bulletin* 106, 74–96.

Anderson, E. (1994). The code of the streets. *Atlantic Monthly* 5, 81–94.

Anderson, M. (1994). Opinion: Banning guns is not the answer, more Americans should carry guns. *For the People News Reporter,* January 10, p. 3.

Archer, D., and Gartner, R. (1984). *Violence and crime in cross-national perspective.* New Haven: Yale University Press.

Ayers, E. L. (1984). *Vengeance and justice.* New York: Oxford University Press.

Bailey, R. (1989). Blacks in northern cities. In Wilson and Ferris (1989).

Baron, L., and Straus, M. A. (1988). Cultural and economic sources of homicide in the United States. *Sociological Quarterly* 29, 371–390.

_____ (1989). *Four theories of rape in American society: A state-level analysis.* New Haven: Yale University Press.

Barone, M., and Ujifusa, G. (1991). *The almanac of American politics 1992.* Washington: National Journal.

Black-Michaud, J. (1975). *Cohesive force: Feud in the Mediterranean.* Oxford: Basil Blackwell.

Blau, J. R., and Blau, P. M. (1982). The cost of inequality: Metropolitan structure and violent crime. *American Sociological Review* 47, 114–129.

Blethen, T., and Wood, C., Jr. (1983). *From Ulster to Carolina: The migration of the Scotch-Irish to southwestern North Carolina.* Cullowhee, N.C.: The Mountain Heritage Center, Western Carolina University.

Blumenthal, M. D., Chadiha, L. B., Cole, G. A., and Jayaratne, T. E. (1975). *More about justifying violence: Methodological studies of attitudes and behavior.* Ann Arbor: University of Michigan, Institute for Social Research.

Blumenthal, M. D., Kahn, R. L., Andrews, F. M., and Head, K. B. (1972). *Justifying violence: Attitudes of American men*. Ann Arbor: University of Michigan, Institute for Social Research.

Bograd, M. (1988). How battered women and abusive men account for domestic violence: Excuses, justifications, or explanations? In G. Hotaling, D. Finkelhor, J. Kirkpatrick, and M. Straus, eds. *Coping with family violence*. Newbury Park, Calif.: Sage Publications.

Booth, A., Shelley, G., Mazur, A., Tharp, G., and Kittok, R. (1989). Testosterone and winning and losing in human competition. *Hormones and Behavior* 23, 556–571.

Brearley, H. C. (1934). The pattern of violence. In W. T. Couch, ed. *Culture in the South*. Chapel Hill: University of North Carolina Press.

Brown, R. M. (1969). The American vigilante tradition. In Graham and Gurr (1969).

Bureau of Justice Statistics (1992). *Capital Punishment 1991*. Washington: Department of Justice.

Campbell, B., O'Rourke, M., and Rabow, M. (1988). Pulsatile response of salivary testosterone and cortisol to aggressive competition in young males. Paper presented at the annual meeting of the American Association of Physical Anthropologists, Kansas City.

Campbell, J. K. (1965). Honour and the devil. In Peristiany (1965).

Carter, H. (1950). *Southern legacy*. Baton Rouge: Louisiana State University Press.

Cash, W. J. (1941). *The mind of the South*. New York: Knopf.

Caudill, H. M. (1962). *Night comes to the Cumberlands*. Boston: Little, Brown.

Center for Political Studies (1979). *The American national election series: 1972, 1974, and 1976*. [Machine-readable data file]. Ann Arbor: Inter-University Consortium for Political and Social Research.

Chadwick, N. (1970). *The Celts*. Hammondsworth, England: Penguin Books.

Chagnon, N. A. (1966). Yanomamo warfare, social organization, and marriage alliances. Unpublished doctoral dissertation, University of Michigan.

Chagnon, N. A. (1968). *Yanomamo, the fierce people*. New York: Holt, Rinehart, and Winston.

⸺⸺⸺ (1974). *Studying the Yanomamo*. New York: Holt, Rinehart, and Winston.

⸺⸺⸺ (1992). *Yanomamo: The last days of Eden*. San Diego: Harcourt Brace Jovanovich.

Cohen, D. (1994). Insult, aggression, and the southern culture of honor: An "experimental ethnography." Unpublished doctoral dissertation, University of Michigan.

⸺⸺⸺ (In press). Law, social policy, and violence: The impact of regional cultures. *Journal of Personality and Social Psychology*.

Cohen, D., and Nisbett, R. E. (1994). Self-protection and the culture of honor: Explaining southern homicide. *Personality and Social Psychology Bulletin* 20, 551–567.

⸺⸺⸺ (1995). Field experiments examining the culture of honor: The role of institutions in perpetuating norms about violence. Manuscript.

Cohen, D., Nisbett, R. E., Bowdle, B., and Schwarz, N. (In press). Insult, aggression, and the southern culture of honor: An "experimental ethnography." *Journal of Personality and Social Psychology*.

Corcoran, J. X. W. P. (1970). Introduction to N. Chadwick, *The Celts*. Hammondsworth, England: Penguin Books.

Cotton, J. L. (1986). Ambient temperature and violent crime. *Journal of Applied Social Psychology* 9, 786–801.

Crèvecoeur, J. H. St. J. ([1782] 1981). *Letters from an American farmer.* Hammondsworth, England: Penguin Books.

Cunliffe, B. (1979). *The Celtic World.* New York: McGraw-Hill.

Dabbs, J. M. (1992). Testosterone measurements in social and clinical psychology. *Journal of Social and Clinical Psychology* 11, 302–321.

Dabbs, J. M., and Hooper, C. H. (1990). Cortisol, arousal, and personality in two groups of normal men. *Personality and Individual Differences* 11, 931–935.

Daly, M., and Wilson, M. (1988). *Homicide.* Hawthorne, N.Y.: Aldine De Gruyter.

Davidson, T. (1977). Wife beating: A recurring phenomenon throughout history. In M. Roy, ed. *Battered Women: A Psychological Study of Domestic Violence.* New York: Nostrand Reinhold.

Davis, J. A., and Smith, T. W. (1990). *General Social Surveys, 1972–1990.* [Machine-readable data file]. Chicago: National Opinion Research Center.

Dobash, R. E., and Dobash, R. P. (1977–1978). Wives: The "appropriate victims of marital violence." *Victimology: An International Journal* 2, 426–442.

Dugger, C. W. (1994). Boy in search of respect discovers how to kill. *New York Times,* May 15, p. 1.

Durkheim, E. (1938). *The rules of sociological method.* New York: Free Press.

Edgerton, R. (1971). *The individual in cultural adaptation.* Berkeley: University of California Press.

Elias, M. (1981). Serum cortisol, testosterone, and testosterone-binding globulin responses to competitive fighting in human males. *Aggressive Behavior* 7, 215–224.

Ellsworth, P. C., and Ross, L. (1983). Public opinion and capital punishment: A close examination of the views of abolitionists and retentionists. *Crime and Delinquency* 29, 116–169.

Evans, R. I. (1970). *Gordon Allport.* New York: E. P. Dutton.

Farb, P. ([1968] 1978). *Man's rise to civilization: The cultural ascent of the Indians of North America.* New York: Penguin.

Fischer, D. H. (1989). *Albion's seed: Four British folkways in America.* New York: Oxford University Press.

Fisek, G. O. (1983). Turkey: Understanding and altering family and political violence. In A. P. Goldstein and M. H. Segall, eds. *Aggression in global perspective.* New York: Pergamon.

Fitzpatrick, R. (1989). *God's frontiersmen: The Scots-Irish epic.* London: Weidenfeld and Nicolson.

Flanagan, T. J., and Jamieson, K. M., eds. (1988). *Sourcebook of criminal justice statistics—1987.* Washington: Department of Justice.

Flanagan, T. J., and McGarrell, E. F., eds. (1986). *Sourcebook of criminal justice statistics—1985.* Washington: Department of Justice.

Flanagan, T. J., and Maguire, K., eds. (1992). *Sourcebook of criminal justice statistics—1991.* Washington: Department of Justice.

Fox, J. A., and Pierce, G. L. (1987). *Uniform crime reports (United States): Supplementary homicide reports, 1976–1983.* [Machine-readable data file]. Ann Arbor: Inter-University Consortium for Political and Social Research.

Franklin, J. H. (1956). *The militant South: 1800–1861.* Cambridge: Harvard University Press.

Frantz, J. B. (1969). The frontier tradition: An invitation to violence. In Graham and Gurr (1969).

Frazier, H. C. (1990). Corporal and capital punishment of juveniles. *International Journal of Medicine and Law,* 9, 996–1004.

Friday, P. C. (1983). Urban crime. In S. H. Kadish, ed. *Encyclopedia of criminal justice.* New York: Free Press.

Galaty, J. G. (1991). The Maasai expansion. In Galaty and Bonte (1991).

Galaty, J. G., and Bonte, P., eds. (1991). *Herders, warriors, and traders: Pastoralism in Africa.* Boulder, Colo.: Westview Press.

Galle, O., Gove, W., and McPherson, J. M. (1972). Population density and social pathology: What are the relationships for man? *Science* 176, 23–30.

Gallup (1981). Gallup Crime Audit. *Gallup Report,* April.

Gastil, R. D. (1971). Homicide and a regional culture of violence. *American Sociological Review* 36, 416–427.

———— (1989). Violence, crime and punishment. In Wilson and Ferris (1989).

Gelles, R. J., and Cornell, C. P. (1990). *Intimate violence in families.* Newbury Park, Calif.: Sage Publications.

Gelles, R. J., and Straus, M. A. (1988). *Intimate violence.* New York: Simon and Schuster.

Gilmore, D. D. (1990). *Manhood in the making: Cultural concepts of masculinity.* New Haven: Yale University Press.

Gillespie, C. K. (1989). *Justifiable homicide.* Columbus: Ohio State University Press.

Gladue, B. A. (1991). Aggressive behavioral characteristics, hormones, and sexual orientation in men and women. *Aggressive Behavior* 17, 313–326.

Gladue, B. A., Boechler, M., and McCaul, K. D. (1989). Hormonal response to competition in human males. *Aggressive Behavior* 15, 409–422.

Gordon, R. A. (1986). Issues in multiple regression. *American Journal of Sociology* 78, 592–616.

Gorn, E. J. (1985). "Gouge, and bite, pull hair and scratch": The social significance of fighting in the southern backcountry. *American Historical Review* 90, 18–43.

Graham, H., and Gurr, T., eds. (1969). *The History of violence in America.* New York: Bantam.

Greenberg, D. F. (1983). Age and crime. In S. H. Kadish, ed. *Encyclopedia of criminal justice.* New York: Free Press.

Gross, S. R. (1993). The romance of revenge: Capital punishment in America. *Studies in Law, Politics, and Society* 13, 71–104.

Gross, S. R., and Mauro, R. (1989). *Death and discrimination.* Boston: Northeastern University Press.

Guerra, N. (In press). Intervening to prevent childhood aggression in the inner city. In J. McCord, ed. *Growing up violent.* New York: Cambridge University Press.

Hackney, S. (1969). Southern violence. *The American Historical Review* 74, 906–925.

Handgun Control Incorporated. (no date a). United States Senate: Voting records on key gun issues (1985–1991). Washington: Handgun Control Incorporated.

Handgun Control Incorporated. (no date b). U.S. House of Representatives: Voting records on key gun issues (1986–1991). Washington: Handgun Control Incorporated.

Harer, M. D., and Steffensmeier, D. (1992). The differing effects of economic inequality on Black and White rates of violence. *Social Forces* 70, 1035–1054.

Harries, K. D. (1974). *The geography of crime and justice.* New York: McGraw-Hill.

———— (1980). *Crime and the environment.* Springfield, Ill.: Charles C. Thomas.

Harries, K. D., and Stadler, S. J. (1988). Heat and violence: New findings from Dallas field data, 1980–1981. *Journal of Applied Social Psychology* 18, 129–138.

Hart, B. (1992). *State codes on domestic violence.* Reno: National Council of Juvenile and Family Court Judges.

Hartz, L. (1969). A comparative study of fragment cultures. In Graham and Gurr (1969).

Hindelang, M. J. (1981). Variations in sex-race-age-specific incidence rates of offending. *American Sociological Review* 46, 461–474.

Hirschi, T., and Gottfredson, M. (1983). Age and the explanation of crime. *American Journal of Sociology* 89, 552–584.

Huesmann, L. R. (1988). An information-processing model for the development of aggression. *Aggressive Behavior* 14, 13–24.

Huff-Corzine, L., Corzine, J., and Moore, D. C. (1986). Southern exposure: Deciphering the South's influence on homicide rates. *Social Forces* 64, 907–924.

Ireland, R. M. (1979). Law and disorder in nineteenth-century Kentucky. *Vanderbilt Law Review* 32, 281–299.

Jackson, J. B. (1972). *American space.* New York: Norton. 65–166. Cited in Gastil, R. (1975). *Cultural regions of the United States.* Seattle: University of Washington Press.

Johnson, S. (1839). *Johnson's English Dictionary.* Philadelphia: Kimber and Sharpless.

Kahn, H. (1968). *On escalation: Metaphors and scenarios.* Baltimore: Penguin Books.

Katz, D. (1960). The functional approach to the study of attitudes. *Public Opinion Quarterly* 24, 163–204.

Katz, D., and Allport, F. H. (1931). *Student attitudes: A report of the Syracuse University research study.* Syracuse, N.Y.: Craftsman Press.

Keegan, J. (1944). *Six armies in Normandy: From D-Day to the liberation of Paris.* New York: Penguin Books.

Kemper, T. D. (1990). *Social structure and testosterone.* New Brunswick: Rutgers University Press.

Kinder, D. R., and Sears, D. O. (1981). Prejudice and politics: Symbolic racism versus racial threats to the good life. *Journal of Personality and Social Psychology* 40, 414–431.

Kirschbaum, C., Bartussek, D., and Strasburger, C. J. (1992). Cortisol responses to psychological stress and correlations with personality traits. *Personality and Individual Differences* 13, 1353–1357.

Kish, L. (1965). *Survey sampling.* New York: Wiley.

Klein, L. R. (1962). *An introduction to econometrics.* Englewood Cliffs, N.J.: Prentice-Hall.

Knauft, B. M. (1991). Violence and sociality in human evolution. *Current Anthropology* 32, 391–428.

Kowalski, G. S., and Peete, T. A. (1991). Sunbelt effects on homicide rates. *Sociology and Social Research* 75, 73–79.

LaFave, W. R., and Scott, A. W. (1986). *Substantive criminal law.* St. Paul: West Publishing Co.

Land, K. E., McCall, P. L., and Cohen, L. E. (1990). Structural covariates of homicide rates: Are there any invariances across time and social space? *American Journal of Sociology* 95, 922–963.

Last ? Resort, The (1990). *Newsletter of the Committee to End Violence Against the Next Generation,* no. 19, Berkeley, Fall.

Lee, R. S. (1993). Machismo values and violence in America. Manuscript.

Leshner, A. I. (1983). Pituitary-adrenocortical effects on intermale agonistic behavior. In B. Svare, ed. *Hormones and Aggressive Behavior.* New York: Plenum Press.

Loftin, C., and Hill, R. H. (1974). Regional subculture and homicide: An examination of the Gastil-Hackney thesis. *American Sociological Review* 39, 14–724.

Loftin, C., and Parker, R. N. (1985). An errors-in-variable model of the effect of poverty on urban homicide rates. *Criminology* 23, 269–287.

Lowie, R. H. (1954). *Indians of the plain.* New York: McGraw-Hill.

Lundsgaarde, H. P. (1977). *Murder in Space City: A cultural analysis of Houston homicide patterns.* New York: Oxford University Press.

Mandelbaum, D. G. (1988). *Women's seclusion and men's honor: Sex roles in North India.* Tucson: University of Arizona Press.

Markus, H. R., and Kitayama, S. (1991). Culture and self: Implications for cognition, emotion and motivation. *Psychological Review* 98, 224–253.

May, R. E. (1989). Fighting South. In Wilson and Ferris (1989).

Mazur, A. (1985). A biosocial model of status in face-to-face primate groups. *Social Forces* 64, 377–402.

Mazur, A., Booth, A., and Dabbs, J. M. (1992). Testosterone and chess competition. *Social Psychology Quarterly* 55, 70–77.

Mazur, A., and Lamb, T. A. (1980). Testosterone, status, and mood in human males. *Hormones and Behavior* 14, 236–246.

McCall, N. (1994). *Makes me wanna holler.* New York: Random House.

McCarthy, J. D., Galle, O. R., and Zimmern, W. (1975). Population density, social structure, and interpersonal violence. *American Behavioral Scientist* 18, 771–791.

McPherson, J. M. (1972). Lacunae in causal model research. Unpublished doctoral dissertation, Vanderbilt University.

McWhiney, G. (1988). *Cracker culture: Celtic ways in the old South.* Tuscaloosa: University of Alabama Press.

Messner, S. F. (1982). Poverty, inequality, and the urban homicide rate. *Criminology* 20, 103–114.

_____ (1983). Regional and racial effects on the urban homicide rate: The subculture of violence revisited. *American Journal of Sociology* 88, 997–1007.

Messner, S. F., and Gordon, R. M. (1992). Racial inequality and racially disaggregated homicide rates: An assessment of alternative theoretical explanations. *Criminology* 30, 421–445.

Miller, D. T., and Prentice, D. A. (1994). Collective errors and errors about the collective. *Personality and Social Psychology Bulletin* 20, 541—550.

Miller, W. I. (1993). *Humiliation.* Ithaca: Cornell University Press.

Mischke, P. E. (1981). Criminal law-homicide-self-defense-duty to retreat. *Tennessee Law Review* 48, 1000–1023.

Mulvihill, D. J., Tumin, M. M., and Curtis, L. A. (1969). *Crimes of violence,* Vol. 11. Washington: U.S. Government Printing Office.

Naipaul, V. S. (1989). *A turn in the South.* New York: Knopf.

Napier, J. (1989). Military tradition. In Wilson and Ferris (1989).

National Center on Women and Family Law (1991, updated 1993). Mandatory arrest summary chart. New York: National Center on Women and Family Law.

National Coalition to Abolish Corporal Punishment in Schools (1993). Corporal punishment bans by state. Columbus: National Coalition to Abolish Corporal Punishment in Schools.

National Rifle Association (1992). *Compendium of state laws governing handguns.* Washington: National Rifle Association.

Nettler, G. (1984). *Explaining crime,* 3d ed. New York: McGraw-Hill.

Nisbett, R. E. (1993). Violence and U.S. regional culture. *American Psychologist* 48, 441–449.

Nisbett, R. E., Polly, G., and Lang, S. (1995). Homicide and U.S. regional culture. In B. R. Ruback and N. A. Weiner, eds. *Interpersonal violent behaviors.* New York: Springer.

Nolan, J. R., and Henry, B. R. (1988). *Massachusetts practice:* Vol. 32, *Criminal law,* 2nd ed. St. Paul: West Publishing Co.

O'Kelley, C. G., and Carney, L. S. (1986). *Women and men in society.* New York: D. Van Nostrand Co.

Oleson, K. C., and Darley, J. M. (1993). Diverging perceptions of excessive counter-aggressive force: The community versus the legal code. Poster session at the 5th Annual Meeting of the American Psychological Society, Chicago.

Olweus, D. (1986). Aggression and hormones: Behavioral relationship with testosterone and adrenaline. In D. Olweus, J. Block, and Marian Radke-Yarrow, eds. *Development of Antisocial and Prosocial Behavior.* Orlando: Academic Press.

Osborne, R. E., Niekrasz, I., and Seale, T. W. (1993). Testosterone induces rapid onset of anxiolytic-like behaviors in mice. Paper presented at Evolution and Human Behavior Meeting, Buffalo.

Parker, R. N. (1989). Poverty, subculture of violence, and type of homicide. *Social Forces* 67, 983–1007.

Parker, R. N., and Smith, M. D. (1979). Deterrence, poverty, and type of homicide. *American Journal of Sociology* 85, 614–624.

Pearson, H. (1994). Black America's silent majority. *New York Times,* May 26, p. A17.

Peristiany, J. G., ed. (1965). *Honour and shame: The values of Mediterranean society.* London: Weidenfeld and Nicolson.

Pitt-Rivers, J. (1965). Honour and social status. In Peristiany (1965).

———— (1968). Honor. In D. Sills, ed. *International encyclopedia of the social sciences.* New York: Macmillan.

Popp, K., and Baum, A. (1989). Hormones and emotions: Affective correlates of endocrine activity. In H. Wagner and A. Manstead, eds. *Handbook of social psychophysiology.* Chichester: John Wiley and Sons.

Popper, F. J., Greenberg, M. R., and Carey, G. W. (1987). Violent death, violent states, and American youth. *Public Interest* 87, 38–48.

Reaves, A. L. (1993). The cultural ecology of rural white homicide in the southern United States. Unpublished doctoral dissertation, University of Michigan.

Reaves, A. L., and Nisbett, R. E. (1995). The cultural ecology of rural white homicide in the southern United States. Manuscript.Redfield, H. V. (1880). *Homicide, North and South: Being a comparative view of crime against the person in several parts of the United States.* Cited in Gastil (1989).

Reed, J. S. (1971). To live—and die—in Dixie: A contribution to the study of southern violence. *Political Science Quarterly* 3, 429–443.

———— (1981). Below the Smith and Wesson line: Reflections on southern violence. In M. Black and J. S. Reed, eds. *Perspectives on the American South: An annual review of society, politics, and culture.* New York: Cordon and Breach Science Publications.

Reifman, A. S., Larrick, R. P., and Fein, S. (1991). Temper and temperature on the diamond: The heat-aggression relationship in major league baseball. *Personality and Social Psychology Bulletin* 17, 580–585.

Robinson, P. H. (1984). *Criminal law defenses.* St. Paul: West Publishing Co.

Rosaldo, M. Z. (1980). *Knowledge and passion: Ilongot notions of self and social life.* New York: Cambridge University Press.

Rosaldo, R. (1980). *Ilongot headhunting, 1883–1974: A study in society and history.* Stanford: Stanford University Press.

Rose, W. L. (1976). *A documentary history of slavery in North America.* New York: Oxford University Press.

Ross, M. H. (1985). Internal and external conflict and violence: Cross-cultural evidence and a new analysis. *Journal of Conflict Resolution* 29, 547–579.

———— (1986). A cross-cultural theory of political conflict and violence. *Political Psychology* 7, 427–469.

Rotton, J., and Frey, J. (1985). Air pollution, weather, and violent crimes: Concomitant time-series analysis of archival data. *Journal of Personality and Social Psychology* 49, 1207–1220.

Salvador, A., Simon, V., Suay, F., and Llorens, L. (1987). Testosterone and cortisol responses to competitive fighting in human males: A pilot study. *Aggressive Behavior* 13, 9–13.

Schelling, T. C. (1963). The threat of violence in international affairs. *Proceedings of the American Society of International Law* (pp. 103–115). Washington: American Society of International Law.

Schmitt, R. C. (1966). Density, health, and social organization. *Journal of the American Institute of Planners* 32, 38–40.

Sears, D. O., and Kinder, D. R. (1971). The good life, white racism, and the Los Angeles voter. In W. Hirsch, ed. *Los Angeles: Viability and prospects for metropolitan leadership.* New York: Praeger.

Shattuck, R. (1989). The reddening of America. *New York Review of Books,* March 30, 3–5.

Shweder, R. A. (1991). *Thinking through cultures.* Cambridge: Harvard University Press.

Siegel, L. J. (1989). *Criminology.* St. Paul: West Publishing Co.

Simpson, M. E. (1985). Violent crime, income inequality, and regional culture: Another look. *Sociological Focus* 18, 199–208.

Sloan, I. J. (1987). *The law of self-defense: Legal and ethical principles.* London: Oceana Publications.

Smith, M. D., and Parker, R. N. (1980). Type of homicide and variation in regional rates. *Social Forces* 59, 136–147.

Snyder, J. R. (1993). A nation of cowards. *Public Interest* 113, 40–55.

Sperber, D. (1991). The epidemiology of beliefs. In C. Fraser and G. Leskell, eds. *The social psychological study of widespread beliefs.* Oxford: Clarendon Press.

Thompson, J. G. (1988). *The psychobiology of emotions.* New York: Plenum Press.

Tocqueville, A. ([1835] 1969). In J. P. Mayer, ed. *Democracy in America,* trans. George Lawrence. Garden City, N.Y.: University of Chicago Press.

Triandis, H. C. (1995). *Individualism and collectivism.* Boulder, Colo.: Westview Press.

U.S. Bureau of the Census (1983). *County and city data book.* Washington: U.S. Government Printing Office.

U.S. Department of Education (1992). 1990 elementary and secondary school civil rights survey. Washington: U.S. Department of Education.

U.S. Department of Justice (1992). *Capital punishment 1991.* Washington: Bureau of Justice Statistics.

U.S. Department of Justice (1984). *Uniform crime reports: U.S. supplementary homicide reports, 1976–1983.*

Will, G. F. (1983). *Statecraft as soulcraft: What government does.* New York: Simon and Schuster.

⸻ (1993). Are we 'a nation of cowards'? *Newsweek,* November 15, 93–94.

Williams, K. R. (1984). Economic sources of homicide: Reestimating the effects of poverty and inequality. *American Sociological Review* 49, 283–289.

Wilson, C. R, and Ferris, W., eds. (1989). *Encyclopedia of southern culture.* Chapel Hill: University of North Carolina Press.

Wilson, W. J. (1987). *The truly disadvantaged.* Chicago: University of Chicago Press.

Winsborough, H. (1970). The social consequences of high population density. In T. Ford and C. DeJong, eds. *Social demography.* Englewood Cliffs, N.J.: Prentice-Hall, 84–90.

Wolfgang, M. E., and Ferracuti, F. (1967). *The subculture of violence.* London: Tavistock Publications.

Wyatt-Brown, B. (1982). *Southern honor: Ethics and behavior in the Old South.* New York: Oxford University Press.

⸻ (1986). *Honor and violence in the Old South.* New York: Oxford University Press.

Zelinsky, W. (1973). *The cultural geography of the United States.* Englewood Cliffs, N.J.: Prentice-Hall.

About the Book and Authors

IN THE UNITED STATES, the homicide rate in the South is consistently higher than the rate in the North. In this brilliantly argued book, Richard Nisbett and Dov Cohen use this fact as a starting point for an exploration of the underlying reasons for violence.

According to Nisbett and Cohen, the increased tendency of white southerners to commit certain kinds of violence is not due to socioeconomic class, population density, the legacy of slavery, or the heat of the South; it is the result of a culture of honor in which a man's reputation is central to his economic survival. Working from historical, survey, social policy, and experimental data, the authors show that in the South it is more acceptable to be violent in response to an insult, in order to protect home and property, and to aid in socializing children. These values are reflected not only in what southerners say, but also in the institutional practices of the South, the actions of southerners, and their physiological responses to perceived affronts.

In this lively and intriguing account, the authors combine bold theory and careful methodology to reveal a set of central beliefs that can contribute to increased violence. More broadly, they show us the interaction between culture, economics, and individual behavior. This engaging study will be of interest to students, educated lay readers, and scholars.

Richard E. Nisbett is Theodore M. Newcomb Distinguished University Professor of Psychology and co-director of the Culture and Cognition Program at the University of Michigan. **Dov Cohen** is assistant professor of psychology at the University of Illinois, Urbana-Champaign.

Index